the teaching of Folk Dance

This is a volume in the Books for Libraries collection

DANCE

See last pages of this volume for a complete list of titles.

the teaching of Folk Dance

ANNE SCHLEY DUGGAN

JEANETTE SCHLOTTMANN

ABBIE RUTLEDGE

BOOKS FOR LIBRARIES
A Division of Arno Press
New York   1980

Editorial Supervision: Janet Byrne

———

Reprint Edition 1980 by Books for Libraries, A Division of Arno
Press Inc.

Copyright © 1948 by A.S. Barnes & Company, Inc.

Reprinted from a copy in the University of Illinois Library
DANCE
ISBN for complete set: 0-8369-9275-X
See last pages of this volume for titles.
Publisher's note: ISBN for 5-vol. *The Folk Dance Library*
0-8369-9305-5

Manufactured in the United States of America

———

Library of Congress Cataloging in Publication Data

Duggan, Anne Schley, 1905-
  The teaching of folk dance.

  (Their The folk dance library ; [v. 1])
  Reprint of the ed. published by A. S. Barnes, New
York.
  Bibliography: p.
  Includes index.
  1. Folk dancing--Study and teaching. I. Schlottmann,
Jeanette, joint author. II. Rutledge, Abbie, joint
author. III. Title.
GV1743.D8 1980 vol. 1   793.3'1s [793.3'1'07]   79-26532
ISBN 0-8369-9283-0

THE TEACHING OF FOLK DANCE

The Folk Dance Library

ANNE SCHLEY DUGGAN

JEANETTE SCHLOTTMANN

ABBIE RUTLEDGE

☆

The Teaching of Folk Dance

Folk Dances of Scandinavia

Folk Dances of European Countries

Folk Dances of the British Isles

Folk Dances of the United States and Mexico

☆

The Folk Dance Library

the teaching of Folk Dance

ANNE SCHLEY DUGGAN
JEANETTE SCHLOTTMANN
ABBIE RUTLEDGE

A. S. BARNES AND COMPANY, NEW YORK

Manufactured in the United States of America.

Dedication

To Stella Owsley, our mutual friend and a genuine lover of the folk arts, who has contributed richly through her aid and encouragement to the preparation of *The Folk Dance Library*—and to our students of folk dance everywhere.

The Authors

Preface

The Folk Dance Library was undertaken by the authors as the result of innumerable requests directed both to them and to the publishers from teachers at all educational levels and from recreation leaders for a presentation of folk dance materials immediately adaptable to the teaching of folk dance as a cultural subject as well as a form of motor activity. It is designed, therefore, to provide teachers of folk dance in schools and colleges, recreationalists, leaders of folk dance in churches and civic organizations, and all individuals everywhere who are interested in this fascinating heritage of our civilization with a more intimate acquaintance with folk dance materials as a means of enriching their study. The underlying purposes of the authors in undertaking the development of *The Folk Dance Library* are:

First, to present a collection of folk dances representative of as many nations as possible with clear directions and musical accompaniments for each of the dances analyzed.

Second, to arrange the folk dances presented in units of organization according to specific geographical regions with representative dances of varying degrees of difficulty within each unit. *The Folk Dance Library* includes the directions and music for eighty-three folk dances grouped into seven regional units for their presentation along with the analyses of fundamental and basic steps, formations, and directions employed in the descriptions of the dances themselves. This organization of materials into units serves the two-fold purpose of providing enough folk dance material to insure more than a sporadic and superficial acquaintance with the characteristic folk dances of the countries represented and of providing enough folk dance material within each unit to serve as a nucleus for folk dance parties, festivals, and other culminating projects. In each unit, therefore, there are some very simple dances for general participation as well as others which will prove challenging for demonstration purposes for those of more advanced skill. The dances listed in each unit are arranged in order of difficulty and include dances for boys and men only, for girls and women only, and for mixed groups comprised of both sexes. The material incorporates dances which are ceremonial and ritualistic in origin as well as those which are highly social and recreational in nature.

Third, to present background materials in conjunction with each unit of dances so that folk dance may be correlated with and integrated more effectively into the curriculum as a whole to the end that, through folk dance, students may gain a better understanding of their neighbors in the world at large. Each unit includes, therefore, (1) a brief resume of the history and characteristics of the peoples whose dances are analyzed; (2) a survey of general topographical and climatic conditions of the given region and a map with the placement of towns, villages, rivers, and mountains directly associated with the origins of the dances which follow; and (3) an overview of the folk dances of the specific country or countries described, significant holidays or festivals commemorated, forms of musical accompaniments, and traditional costumes with a colored costume plate illustrating authentic and typical costumes

7

worn by dancers of the particular region in question. Wherever possible, the origins of the individual dances comprising each unit are pointed out with respect to the significance of their titles, formations, and basic steps. This background material is necessarily brief but suggestive of a wealth of information which, properly utilized, is significant because it is reflected in the dances themselves and should insure, therefore, the teaching of folk dance as a folk art. The bibliographies included in each of the volumes provide sources for further study.

Fourth, to foster a vitalized feeling of nationalism in every country and to demonstrate through folklore the close cultural ties shared by the peoples of all nations, thereby promoting a broader concept of internationalism.

Fifth, to indoctrinate boys and girls and men and women everywhere with the idea that participation in the folk dances of all countries is an indispensable phase of their education, affording not only invaluable training in rhythm and basic motor skills but also the means of realizing all sorts of concomitant or associated learnings as well—folklore, legends, customs, costumes, traditions, holidays and feast days, folk songs, folk music and other related arts—to the end that folk dance may serve as an enriching, leisure-time activity for those of all ages.

The Folk Dance Library consists of five volumes variously entitled *The Teaching of Folk Dance*, *Folk Dances of Scandinavia*, *Folk Dances of European Countries*, *Folk Dances of the British Isles*, and *Folk Dances of the United States and Mexico*. In preparing the manuscript for *The Teaching of Folk Dance*, the purpose of the authors was to summarize and to apply to the field of folk dance—rather than to duplicate in any sort of technical detail—available materials in educational methodology including those in the special field of testing. Fundamental principles for the production of folk festivals and folk dance parties as culminating projects in conjunction with the folk dance program in schools, colleges, and recreation centers are listed with suggestive outlines for the production of two illustrative folk festivals and a typical folk dance party. This particular book in the series of five volumes was planned, therefore, as an overview to folk dance leadership to be used in conjunction with each of the remaining four volumes comprising *The Folk Dance Library*.

This collection of folk dances is the result of many years of study and firsthand experience with ethnological groups in Mexico and in all parts of this country. It includes, therefore, some folk dances that are old favorites appearing in other collections and a number of dances which have not been published previously. The authors have endeavored throughout to present authentic versions of the folk dances analyzed and to describe them in such a way that they will be interpreted and danced in the manner of tne ethnic groups from whom they were learned. Wherever versions presented differ from those appearing in other collections, the reader is reminded that folk dance, like language, often gives rise to variations in the same manner in which dialects vary in different sections of a given country.

The authors wish to express their gratitude to the many individuals who have contributed through their aid and encouragement to the development of *The Folk Dance Library*. Specifically, they are deeply indebted to Mary Campbell, Texas State College for Women, and to Esther Allen Bremer, Teachers College, Columbia University, for their accurate recording of the various folk melodies accompanying the dances and for their arrangements of these melodies into the piano accompaniments for the dances analyzed; to the two gifted artists at the Texas State College for Women who contributed the illustrations which add immeasurably to the purpose of *The Folk Dance Library* as a whole—Lura B. Kendrick for the colored pictorial maps and for the colored costume plates for each unit and Coreen Spellman for the brush drawings, black and white maps, and illustrative diagrams; to the historians on the faculty of the Texas State College for Women who read the sections devoted to geographical, historical, and sociological background material for the various units; to June Anderson and Claire Mae Jenkins, major students in the Department of Health, Physical Education, and Recreation of the Texas State College for Women for their service as patient and skillful models for the illustrators; and to Bette Jean Reed for her invaluable assistance in the preparation of the manuscript. The authors are grateful to the publishers who have granted permission for the use of direct quotations.

It is the sincere hope of the authors that *The Folk Dance Library* will prove a source of aid to those whose needs were anticipated in its purposes, and that folk dance will become a living and enriching folk art to boys and girls as well as to men and women everywhere.

ANNE SCHLEY DUGGAN
JEANETTE SCHLOTTMANN
ABBIE RUTLEDGE
Texas State College for Women, Denton, Texas

9

Table of Contents

The Teaching of Folk Dance

Pronunciation of Foreign Words

The list of words given below includes all those foreign words which appear in this volume—*The Teaching of Folk Dance*—and which may not be found in *Webster's Collegiate Dictionary*, Fifth Edition, in the section devoted to English words, in the Pronouncing Gazeteer, or in the Pronouncing Biographical Dictionary. The pronunciations given here approximate the foreign pronunciations as closely as is possible with English vowels and consonants.

The following symbols establish the pronunciation of the vowel and consonant sounds in the various words included in the list and appear in italics within the syllables of each word:

a as in t*a*g
ah as in f*a*ther
ain as in br*an*ch
e as in m*e*t
ee as in p*ee*k
eh as in p*a*y
ei as in th*ey*'re
g as in *g*et

zh as in a*z*ure

i as in h*i*t
ie as in p*ie*
o as in l*o*ss
oh as in m*o*re
oo as in f*oo*d
oun as in s*on*g
ow as in n*ow*
uh as in *u*p

Adelita—*Ah*-d*eh*-l*ée*-t*ah*
adiós—*ah*-d*ee*-*óh*s
Alameda—*Ah*-l*ah*-m*éh*-d*ah*
Arbeau—*Ar*-b*oh*
Bienvenidos Todos—B*ee*-*éh*n-v*eh*-n*ée*-d*oh*s
    T*óh*-d*oh*s
binjou—b*ain*-*zhoo*
charro—ch*áh*r-r*oh*
china poblana—ch*ée*-n*ah*- p*ohb*-l*áh*-n*ah*
corridos—k*oh*r-r*ée*-d*oh*s
Csárdás—ch*ár*-d*ah*sh
Csébogar—ch*éh*-b*oh*-g*ar*
Dal—D*ah*l
diana—d*ee*-*áh*-n*ah*
El Santo Señor de Chalma—*Eh*l-S*áh*n-t*oh*
    S*eh*n-y*óh*r d*eh* Ch*áh*l-m*ah*
Feiar—F*íe*-yu*h*r
Feis—F*eh*sh
fiesta—f*ee*-*éh*s-t*ah*
Floralia—Fl*oh*-r*áh*l-*eeah*
Gomme—G*o*m

Gustaf's Skoal—G*óo*s-t*ahf*'s Sk*oh*l
Hambo—H*ám*-b*oh*
huapango—w*ah*-p*áh*ng-*oh*
huaraches—w*ah*-r*áh*-ch*eh*s
Jabado—*Zha*-b*a*-d*oh*
Jalisco—H*ah*-l*ée*s-k*oh*
Jarabe Tapatío—H*ah*-r*áh*-b*eh* T*ah*-p*ah*-t*ée*-*oh*
jarana—H*ah*-r*áh*-n*ah*
Kolo—k*o*-l*o*
Koróboushka—k*ah*-r*ó*-b*oo*sh-k*ah*
Kynkkaliepakko—K*ín*-k*ah*-l*i*-p*áh*-k*oh*
La Boudigueste—L*a* B*oo*-d*ee*-g*e*st
La Cucaracha—L*ah* K*oo*-k*ah*-r*áh*-ch*ah*h
La Jesucita—L*ah* H*eh*-s*oo*-s*ée*-t*ah*
ländler—l*án*t-l*ei*r
langeleik—l*áh*ng-*eh*-l*eh*k
La Sandunga—L*ah* S*ah*n-d*óo*n-g*ah*
Las Igüiris—L*ah*s E*e*-gw*ée*-rees
Lauterbach—L*ów*-t*ei*r-b*ah*kh
La Virgencita—L*ah*-V*ee*r-h*eh*n-s*ée*-t*ah*

13

La Virgen de Guadalupe — *Lah Véer-hehn deh Gwah-dah-lóo-peh*

Le Stoupic — *Luh Stoo-peek*

Los Matlanchines — *Lohs Maht-lahn-chée-nehs*

Los Viejitos — *Lohs Vee-eh-hée-tohs*

Noche Mexicana — *Nóh-cheh Meh-hee-káh-nah*

Oppé — *O-peh*

Paseo — *Pah-séh-oh*

pasos dobles — *páh-sohs dóhb-lehs*

piñata — *peen-yáh-tah*

Polska — *Póhl-skuh*

ranchero — *rahn-chéh-roh*

Ril — *Ril*

Saludos, Amigos — *Sah-lóo-dohs Ah-mée-gohs*

sarape — *sah-ráh-peh*

Schuhplattler — *Shóo-plaht-leir*

Sur le Pont D'Avignon — *Soor luh Pount Da-vin-youn*

varsovienne — *var-so-vyen*

Vingakers — *Víng-oh-kuhrs*

Viva México — *Vée-vah Méh-hee-koh*

vivas — *vée-vahs*

Vuillier — *Vwee-yeh*

Weggis — *Véh-gis*

zapateado — *sah-pah-teh-áh-doh*

THE TEACHING OF FOLK DANCE

Chapter I
Definition and Sources of Folk Dance

The term *folk dance* should be definitive enough in itself to preclude the necessity for further clarification. Obviously it means the indigenous dances of any specific "folk" and implies that they are evolved and handed down traditionally in the same manner in which genuine folk music, festivals, customs, and costumes are perpetuated.

Over a period of many years, however, the terms *folk dance*, *national dance*, and *character* or *characteristic dance* have been used loosely, interchangeably, and often incorrectly, giving rise to confusion in the basic terminology employed in this area of our folk arts. During the first enthusiasm for programs of physical education in this country, collections entitled *Folk and National Dances* appeared from time to time, including dances that were not traditional in nature, which were utilized as basic texts for courses similarly titled in the catalogues of various teacher education institutions. In more recent years, a new controversy has arisen with respect to *when* a folk dance may be so designated, introducing the idea that contemporary performers may consciously develop their own innovations which will be recognized as traditional in years to come. In view of this confusion in terminology and philosophy, definitions which have governed the inclusion of dances comprising the present *Folk Dance Library* seem advisable. They are in accordance with those advocated by various dance historians, recognized authorities in the field of folk dance, and leaders of ethnological groups with whom the authors have been closely associated.

What then *is* a *folk dance*—a *national dance*—a *character dance* in folk costume and idiom? These definitions are best derived from an understanding of the origins and essential characteristics of the types of dance so designated.

THE FOLK DANCE

Folk dances may be defined as the traditional dances of a given country which have evolved naturally and spontaneously in conjunction with the everyday activities and experiences of the peoples who developed them. Beginning with primitive man, they became the overt expression of emotions and ideas which were peculiarly significant or the re-enactment of customs and events constituting an important part of their history and patterns of daily living. Thus folk dances are related in origin to everything of importance in the daily lives of a specific people at given times in their history, stemming from customs, beliefs, emotions, and events related to religion, war, occupations, ceremonies of birth, courtship, marriage, death, daily activities of domestic life, superstitions, rituals, festivals, and innumerable themes common to all peoples everywhere. They afford, therefore, a vivid and graphic link with the past in which contemporary man had his own beginnings.

We are told by such authorities as G. Stanley Hall that a member of one primitive tribe, upon meeting a member of an alien tribe, asked a single question — "What do you dance?" He might well have asked, "How do you worship? How do you rear and educate your children? What battles have you waged and won? What plagues have you suffered? How do you play? What do you grow and eat?" But the responses to these many questions which might have been posed in an effort to further acquaintance between those of different tribes were unnecessary in that the answer to the single and initial question, "What do you dance?" sufficed for all because it revealed them all.

In tracing the origins of folk dances to definite thematic sources, the problem becomes confusing because of the overlapping of several themes within a single dance in some instances. This is particularly true of the dances of primitive man because of his complete integration resulting in a fusion of the many facets of his life.

Religion is among the pre-eminent sources of origin for the genesis of dance, and the relationship between dance and religion may be traced to a period before history began. The people of ancient times and places danced to conciliate their gods, devising movement to represent some phase of the histories and work of the gods or simply to express their joy as worshipers. They developed special sacrificial dances characterized by an austere and solemn quality as well as wild and weird dances either to propitiate or to frighten away evil spirits. Their sun and seasonal dances were a means of celebrating the conquest of the powers of light over those of darkness and were re-enacted each year at the approach of spring. Their harvest dances were a form of thanksgiving to the gods for the crops garnered at this particular season. Thus many of the folk dances of contemporary nations are modern vestiges of ancient religious rites although the special significance of these sources of origin have been lost in many instances.

The dances of the Indians — and of certain other contemporary primitive tribes — in their solicitation to their gods for rain or sun, for deliverance from illness or pestilence, and for success in warfare are fairly obvious in their religious implications. But how many contemporary folk dancers know that a number of the English country dances also grew out of ancient religious rituals? How many of them know the significance of the accessory figures in English folk festivals — the Jack-in-the-Green, the Hobby Horse, the Fool? These figures, still retained to add humorous and grotesque touches to the public performance of English folk dances, can be traced to their original representation or identification with the plant and animal world, respectively, in the case of the Jack-in-the-Green and the Hobby Horse. The Fool was first introduced to represent a semidivine leader in ancient religious rites; many of the patterns and figures of the dances themselves evolved from pagan religious rituals.

Other examples of the religious origin of the folk dances of various peoples may be found in such familiar singing games of the Western Hemisphere as *London Bridge is Falling Down* and in the dances of the Whirling Dervishes of the Eastern Hemisphere. In the former, we recognize the symbolism of the bridge as the connecting link between life in the present and that in the hereafter. Whether or not this traditional association of bridges may be linked with the Biblical references to the River of Jordan, giving rise to such familiar hymns as

Shall We Gather at the River, and to such poems as Tennyson's *Crossing the Bar* — all commemorative of the passage from this life to the next — is a matter of conjecture. There is considerable evidence, however, for the belief that bridges held a sacred and vital place in the lives of all folk in the early days of their respective histories and that they were chosen, therefore, as the settings of various important events.[1] Thus in *London Bridge is Falling Down*, each participant makes his choice between a lemon and an orange, a diamond and an emerald, in lining up behind the two leaders forming the bridge or arch for the tug of war with which this popular singing game concludes; traditionally, this climax portended the destiny of each player with respect to his ultimate salvation or destruction. Best known, perhaps, of the many bridge dances of France is another singing game entitled *Sur le Pont d'Avignon*.

The dances of the Whirling Dervishes are illustrative of those of many peoples who, under the stimulus of religious inspiration, are enabled to whirl and dance for hours and even days without cessation. We see the survival of dance as a phase of religious expression among various contemporary sects including the Shakers and both Negro and white church denominations known colloquially as Holy Rollers. Individuals among these groups manifest the extent to which they have been moved spiritually by the ecstasy with which they dance. The processionals and recessionals which mark the beginning and end of the religious services of a number of modern orthodox churches are, in reality, a survival of the religious dances of a former period when the priest led the chorus into the church where the choir chancel was designated as the place for the performance of dances included as a definite part of the church ritual.

War has been the theme responsible for the evolution of a number of folk dances taught at elementary, secondary, and college levels in educational institutions. The war dances of the American Indian and of other native tribes, accompanied by the inflammatory beating of drums and the cries of the participants, served originally as preparation for attacks upon their enemies in that courage and strength were augmented thus to a desirable pitch of frenzy. In the performance of their war dances, members of these tribes often anticipated in movement and in pantomime what they expected to happen to their enemies. The theme of war was fused often with that of religion when they appealed to the gods in dance for victorious outcomes in their hostilities. Other dances associated with warfare were performed by women, children, and aged men of various tribes in the absence of the warriors as a prayer for their safe return; upon the return of the warriors, members of the various tribes danced as a part of the funeral rites of those lost in battle as well as in celebration of victorious encounters.

Many of the weapon dances of primitive man and those of later periods in civilization, such as the Pyrrhic dances of Sparta during the height of the period of Grecian culture, were essentially war dances to which may be traced folk dances of various nations based upon the idea of conflict as a fundamental theme. Particularly interesting in their contrast are two Scottish dances stemming from this source—the *Scottish Sword Dance* and the *Highland Fling*. The former, first danced on the eve of battle, called for great agility and ingenuity on the part of the performer when a slip or the touching of the crossed swords around which he

---

[1]Mary Effie Shambaugh, *Folk Dances for Boys and Girls* (New York: A. S. Barnes and Company, 1929), p. 18.

danced was interpreted as an evil omen for the next day's encounter. The *Highland Fling*, on the other hand, was first danced in celebration of victory and performed, therefore, after a successful battle. Both the *Sword Dance* and the *Highland Fling* are danced today in conjunction with Scottish festivals when dancers compete in their performance. A vestige of the importance attached to accuracy of execution on the part of the primitive Scots is found in these festivals when participants are disqualified if they touch the swords crossed on the ground during the performance of their *Sword Dance*.

Also illustrative of war as the original thematic source of familiar folk dances is the English singing game entitled *The Roman Soldiers*. This may be traced to the ancient encounter between the Romans and the early Britons during the first century when the former invaded the British Isles in the extension of the Roman Empire.

The animal dances of primitive man were the antecedents of a wealth of folk dances which are popular among many national groups today. Various tribes of American Indians continue to perform their Buffalo, Deer, Caribou, and Eagle Dances in imitation of the movements, habits, and sounds of these and other animals and fowls which played an important part in their daily living. Less obvious in their animal origins, however, are many popular folk dances which evolved from similar sources such as the *Schuhplattlers* of Bavaria, first danced in imitation of the mating of birds. The ultimate origins of these and other folk dances, stemming from the imitation of animals and of birds, have grown obscure with the inevitable changes effected when traditional dances are handed down from generation to generation.

The animal dances of primitive man, in which he re-enacted all of the movements of the chase as he stalked and killed his prey, were, in a sense, the forerunners of innumerable folk dances based upon work themes in that such dances were related to one of primitive man's chief sources of sustenance. Work or occupational dances grew and flourished with the Trade Guilds of the Middle Ages. Each Guild wove the motifs of its trade into a dance so that today we have folk dances of the shoemaker, the tailor, the cooper, the weaver, the baker, the farmer, the blacksmith, the butcher. Between the fourteenth and fifteenth centuries, these different Trade Guilds — predecessors of our modern unions — had established days for the celebration of their particular occupations during which the performance of their trade dances was an outstanding feature. In their original forms, these dances were so characteristic of the particular occupations represented through movement and pantomime that they were easily recognized as such. In many instances, they were accompanied by the singing of words which also portrayed the occupation in question. Other occupational dances evolved naturally and spontaneously in conjunction with the everyday work activities of individuals and of groups in various countries and constitute a means of gaining insight with respect to how various folk peoples have worked as well as played. *Jolly is the Miller*, a familiar "mixer" among simple American folk dances, is illustrative of an occupational theme in its origin. The disparaging reference to the miller's proverbial dishonesty with "one hand in the hopper and the other in the sack" adds a note of humor and enjoyable reality to folk dancing which, too often, is taught as an artificial activity, superimposed —

not discovered and enjoyed by the student. Further illustrations of occupational folk dances are the American *The Farmer's in the Dell*, the Swedish *Reap the Flax*, the Norwegian *Feiar* or *Chimney Sweep*, the Czechoslovakian *Little Butcher* and others too numerous for listing.

Because some of our occupational folk dances have retained their literal, pantomimic qualities, their performance has been relegated primarily to the elementary school level. There are many delightful ones which are danced by the adults in the countries in which they were developed. They have evolved into simple couple dances, decidedly social in nature, with the waltz or the polka a predominating step pattern. Geary[1] and Shambaugh[2] have included a number of these occupational dances in their respective collections which are enjoyed by mixed groups of young people and adults.

From the time of primitive man, dance has played a vital part in such special ceremonies as courtship, marriage, and death as well as in the domestic activities of every day life including the observation of superstitious beliefs. These themes, in turn, recur in many folk dances of various nations. For example, the ancient custom of searching for a wife is the theme for *Here Come Three Dukes A-Riding*. The lovely Norwegian *Spring Dance* is really a courtship dance in which the man tries to win the admiration of his partner by his display of skill and grace. The Swedish *Dal Dance* portrays woman's subjugation when she kneels for the man's foot to be swung over her head but it also reveals his susceptibility to her coquetry in another figure of the dance. The "eternal triangle" is the theme of *Vingakers Dance* from the same country.

Illustrative of the folk dances commemorative of everyday activities in the domestic life of a people is the childhood favorite *Here We Go Round the Mulberry Bush* and an endless number of dances whose titles are indicative of animals, fowls, insects, and activities which play an important part in the daily lives of a particular group of people such as *La Cucaracha* or "The Cockroach" in Mexico. The Danish *Nixie Polka* exemplifies the superstitious belief in a nixie or water sprite thought to appear at certain times during the year, compelling human beings before whom he danced to follow him.

Space does not permit a more extensive treatment of folk dance origins. The foregoing are illustrative of the wealth of literature available to those encouraged to seek it out. The background material preceding each of the units of folk dances which follow in the four remaining volumes of *The Folk Dance Library* includes further elaboration of the folk dances of each specific country or group of countries comprising these units.

Genuine *folk dances*, therefore, are traditional dances handed down from generation to generation in the manner of all traditions. They are more or less fixed in their basic patterns, but may evince variations in different provinces or sections of the given country in the same manner in which a basic language reveals different dialects and colloquialisms or an original common language undergoes changes over a period of many years. The significant fact, however, is that there has been no conscious effort to introduce such changes or variations. They have come about through repetition in the handing-down process in much the

---

[1]Marjorie Crane Geary, *Folk Dances of Czechoslovakia* (New York: A. S. Barnes and Company, 1927).
[2]Shambaugh, *op. cit.*

same way in which an original sentence whispered from player to player in our childhood game of "Gossip" undergoes many changes in this process of repetition.

THE NATIONAL DANCE

National dances are also traditional folk dances and differ from the latter only in that they are national in scope — that is, they are those folk dances which are most popular and widely danced in all parts of a specific country. While each country may have innumerable folk dances, some of which are unknown in other sections — depending upon the specificity of theme and source or upon geographical conditions and subsequent facilities of communication — each country recognizes as its national dance the one particular folk dance which is the most popular and universally danced in all sections. The Kinneys subscribe to this definition when they refer thus to the *Tarantella*, national dance of Italy: "It is the *Tarantella* that the world at large accepts as Italy's national dance; and rightly enough, since there is none whose popularity is more nearly general through the land."[1]

According to this criterion of a national dance, it is understandable that all countries do not recognize a single dance as national in scope. Illustrative of such dances, however, are the *Tarantella* of Italy, the *Hambo* of Sweden, the *Csárdás* of Hungary, the *Jarabe Tapatío* of Mexico, the *Kolo* of Serbia, the *Schuhplattlers* of Bavaria. It is interesting to note further that many of the folk dances generally recognized as the national dances of various countries share a characteristic common to all. While they may be recorded in a definite sequence of steps for purposes of logic and convenience, they are actually danced in various parts of the particular country without this established sequence of specific steps and with considerable variation as to the inclusion of certain steps from a much larger number of possibilities.

THE CHARACTER DANCE

And finally, how shall we define that third and last type of so-called "folk and national dances" which are *not* traditional in nature, but which someone has created by fitting characteristic steps and designs to the folk melodies of a particular country? For lack of a better name, these may well be called *character dances* rather than folk or national dances. Their origins should be pointed out always to groups to whom they are taught, and the fact made clear that no one can create a folk or national dance since such deliberate creation generally is recognized as diametrically opposed to the true concept of folk and national dances.

SUMMARY

Folk dances may be defined as the traditional dances of a given country which have evolved naturally and spontaneously in conjunction with the everyday activities and experiences of the peoples who developed them, perpetuated from generation to generation in the manner of all traditions. *National dances* are those traditional folk dances which are most popular and widely danced in all parts of a specific country. *Character dances* have been created by a

[1] Margaret and Troy West Kinney, *The Dance* (New York: Tudor Publishing Co., 1935), p. 158.

specific individual or a group of individuals who have fitted characteristic steps and designs to the folk songs or melodies of a particular country.

Chapter 2
Objectives for the Teaching of Folk Dance

When physical education programs were first introduced into this country, they consisted primarily of gymnastics or calisthenic exercises imported from other countries without any genuine attempt to adapt them to the real needs and interests of American youth. Somewhat later, these adopted programs of gymnastics were augmented by folk dances borrowed from the same national sources. Because teachers of this period, however, were preoccupied with formal, precise, and highly regimented methods of presentation in keeping with a formal program of physical education and with objectives based, in the main, upon physiological outcomes, wholly natural folk dance materials were utilized primarily as an additional means of providing physical exercise and presented, therefore, with the same formal method governing the use and underlying purposes of gymnastics. As a result, folk dance for many years was a relatively colorless activity which failed to catch the imagination of the boys and girls to whom it was taught and, as a consequence, became so unpopular that it failed to hold its rightful place for a time in the physical education curriculums of our schools and colleges. Benighted teachers chose folk dance materials which were inappropriate for the group taught. They committed a further error in that they presented long, ritualistic folk dances without giving their proper significance in terms of origin and setting and without any motivation other than that of daily class routine. This use of natural, spontaneous, and colorful folk dance materials as a sterile and stereotyped form of exercise, with emphasis upon physiological results only, sounded a logical death-knell to a vital folk art in educational institutions for a period of many years. Shambaugh epitomized the contrast in objectives for the teaching of folk dance as a form of exercise and as a living folk art when she wrote:

> "To some, the study of folk dancing is only the silhouette; only the study of movement. To others, the study of folk dancing is a vivid picture of national life with a colorful, fanciful background of folk custom, costume, art, music and legend."[1]

No one can challenge the physiological values of folk dance. It affords excellent opportunities for the rhythmic exercise of the muscles, increased respiration and circulation, development of organic vigor and numerous other obviously desirable outcomes of physical activity. In fact, folk dance is a splendid medium for the achievement of the widely recognized fitness objectives of endurance, strength, flexibility, body control — including agility, coordination, and balance — relaxation, and morale.[2] Those who scoff at its potentialities in this regard need only the experience of an evening of folk dance to be convinced. While the physiological

---

[1]Mary Effie Shambaugh, *Folk Festivals* (New York: A. S. Barnes and Company, 1932), p. vii.
[2]Report of the United States Office of Education Committee on Wartime Physical Fitness for Colleges and Universities, *Physical Fitness for Students in Colleges and Universities* (Washington, D. C.: United States Government Printing Office, 1943), pp. 62–64.

values of folk dance, therefore, are fairly irrefutable, and while it is true that these same values may be derived from any one of several equally vigorous motor activities, it is also true that folk dance — when properly taught — affords invaluable outcomes which cannot be duplicated by other aspects of the physical education program. It is upon these outcomes, emanating from the inherent values of folk dance as an educational and recreational activity, that the authors wish to focus the attention of its present and potential teachers.

Many educational leaders have said that the value of education lies primarily in the lasting interests and satisfactions that it brings. Briggs, in his excellent discussion of interests, maintains that an important index of one's education is the number, depth, and extent of one's interests.[1] William Lyon Phelps in his delightful little book called *Happiness* — and happiness in its real, worthwhile sense as satisfaction is doubtless a legitimate and ultimate goal of all living — further links interests with happiness when he defines the happiest man as the man who thinks the most interesting thoughts. If the development and pursuit of active, thoroughgoing, and alive interests is accepted as a basic goal in education, it is important to explore the potentialities of folk dance in this regard and to establish very tangible and, at the same time, broad and far-reaching objectives with respect to its contributions to the achievement of this goal.

Folk dance as an activity in programs of physical education and of recreation affords values rich in possibilities for promoting enduring interests and the satisfactions which attend enriched living. These values in folk dance, extending beyond the realm of good physical exercise, may be grouped, for purposes of a quick overview, into three broad categories: *cultural values*, or those outcomes which awaken interest in and enhance appreciation of the aesthetic aspects of human experience; *social and recreational values*, or those outcomes which help to orient the individual to his role as a member of society and to discipline him in the performance of that role; and *neuromuscular values*, or those outcomes which contribute to the good performance of a well-coordinated body in movement.

CULTURAL VALUES

Cultural values which may result from folk dance when it is properly taught are many and touch a number of facets of human experience. A study of the folk dances of any given country will reveal characteristic types of step patterns and qualities of movement. Study of the folk dances of many countries will facilitate a comparison of movement patterns and will provide clues to differences in temperament and to points of view on the part of the peoples of these countries; subtle differences among groups in the performance of the same step patterns and traditional dance forms may be observed. Paralleling the learning of folk dances of various countries should be a study of the history of folk dance with respect to origins, symbolism, and development which is, in turn, inextricably linked with the history and philosophy of all dance including that at its highest cultural level — dance as an art form.

Closely related to folk dance is folk music, an expression through another medium of the character and temperament of folk peoples. An introduction to the folk music of a given coun-

[1]Thomas H. Briggs, *Secondary Education* (New York: The Macmillan Company, 1933), p. 499.

26

try in conjunction with the teaching of specific folk dances should be directed toward an awareness of the dynamic quality and mood of the musical accompaniments involved and the characteristic rhythmic patterns which prevail. Further study may lead to an appreciation of the history and development of musical accompaniment for folk dances and the typical instruments which supply the background for the dances themselves. Here again, the development of folk music is closely associated with the development of music as a fine art. Folk dances provide some of the clearest examples of generally accepted musical forms so that an understanding of the structure of compositions in this area of the fine arts may be achieved through participation in comparable folk dance forms.

A study of the authentic folk costumes of a country is conducive to a closer understanding of the lives of the people represented and to an appreciation of their respective folk cultures. The history and function of their costumes and the symbolism of color, cut, design, and specific accessories are particularly fascinating approaches to a study of the peoples of any foreign country; for example, the fact that, in several countries, the traditional attire for matrons differs from that of unmarried girls so that young men may know more readily whom they may court with impunity is a unique and pragmatic approach to the problem of social and romantic relationships. Comparable distinctions with respect to differences and potential conflicts through religious beliefs are made also, in some instances, through traditional folk costumes. For example, in certain provinces in France, the large, upright bows which the women wear on their heads are brightly colored if they are Catholics and black if they are Protestants.

Every country affords a wealth of what is generally termed folklore including interesting superstitions, legends, rituals, customs, celebrations, and festivals. These traditional practices of folk peoples throughout the world constitute an exciting and romantic approach to the study and keener appreciation of them and a resultant desire to know more about them.

Through the folk dances of a specific country, students find that they are also studying the geography of the country in which the people of a particular region live. An explanation of the title of the *Highland Fling* immediately presents a mental picture of the contrasting highland and lowland regions of Scotland. The song which accompanies the *Weggis Dance* tells of the lakes of Switzerland and the proximity of the two villages of Lucerne and Weggis and of their respective locations on the shores of Lake Lucerne. The influence of the physical environment with respect to the climate and topography of a specific country upon the development of its folk dances is further exemplified in the short-stepped, level, and somewhat compressed polka of the Czechoslovakians and of other Central European peoples; the light, delicate, springing steps of the Tyroleans; the vigorous and sturdy dances of the Scandinavians; and the slow, languorous figures of some of the dances from Latin-American countries.

Other folk dances reflect historical events which have influenced the lives of the people; for example, Poland's sad history is reflected in the subdued, quiet grace and plaintive quality of some of its folk dances in contrast to the turbulent, stormy qualities of others. Sociological implications, including those of national temperament, are apparent in still other dances which have developed from the local mores of the particular group from which they have evolved. Thus the English country dances evince a smooth, reserved quality, wholly free from

27

affectations of any sort. This same quality, in turn, is reflected in the early American folk dances of New England in contrast to those developed later in the western part of the United States when the rugged individualism of those pioneers, who thrust back the frontiers of this particular section of the country, resulted in a style of folk dance more compatible with their lusty, enthusiastic temperaments and ways of living. *Gustaf's Skoal* is illustrative of the Swedish people's partly serious, partly jesting attitude toward their king. Thus the Swedish peasants developed a dance in two distinct parts; the first part is symbolic of their reverence for their monarch, danced in the form of a solemn salute on the part of devoted subjects while the second part, symbolic of their submission to this yoke of authority, finishes with a carefree, whirling turn as these same subjects laugh at their own submission.

Through these illustrative examples of the geographical, historical, and sociological implications of the folk dances of various nations, it is obvious that a more thorough study may prove a highly valuable medium for the promotion of a genuine sort of internationalism indispensable if peoples of all nations are to live amicably in an atomic age. An English Morris dancer of a former decade observed astutely, "Ye canna fight a man ye've danced wi'." Folk dance is indeed a universal language through which all peoples everywhere may converse together; through folk dance experiences, directed in conjunction with other closely associated aspects of folklore, individuals may become aware of common roots in their heritages as well as of the differences evolving from these generic beginnings. Such awareness is a first step toward a sympathetic understanding of those who live in countries outside of one's own national boundaries. Paradoxically enough, folk dance, under wise leadership, may contribute both to national pride and vitality as well as to international unity.

The study of folk dances is closely related to the various folk arts of a given group — crafts, pottery, wood-carving, leather work and embroidery. A knowledge of folk cultures enables an individual to recognize and to appreciate more completely the use of folk themes as they occur in literature, painting, music, sculpture, and dance, thereby providing the individual with a richer background for appreciation which, in turn, leads into the fine arts developed by various countries.

A final, and an especially important, cultural value which an individual may realize through an acquaintance with folk dance is an appreciation of the contributions of various countries to the growth of the humanities in all nations with respect to song and dance forms and to the celebration of festivals which are either strictly indigenous or shared by all peoples everywhere. The study of these overt expressions of a people establishes a feeling of kinship and engenders a desire for better understanding. Without doubt, when folk dance is properly taught, the result is a joyful participation in—rather than a slightly amused and condescending tolerance of—the folk dances and customs of fellow citizens of the world.

SOCIAL AND RECREATIONAL VALUES

Chief among the social values resulting from a well-directed study of folk dance is the mitigation of a narrow sort of provincialism which often emanates from a mistaken sense of loyalty to one's own country on the part of young people as well as of their elders. This is an especially important outcome if the peoples of all nations are to begin to think in terms of "One World" or of one society of people in all parts of the world. Students should develop, as a result of soundly conducted folk dance experiences, a keener awareness of their positions as individual citizens of a specific country and, at the same time, as members of an organic group — society in the world at large. The discipline of dancing with a small class group can contribute to this awareness and help to shape the concept of the principles involved through a deepened appreciation of the contributions of all nations to a basic folk culture which is shared by all. Students can readily see the importance of conducting themselves reliably as members of a folk dance group when such participation is indispensable to the integrity of a successful performance and the subsequent satisfaction of the group as a whole. Certainly the extension of folk dance as a recreational pursuit, including not only indigenous dances but those of other national groups as well, can further the needed understanding between the peoples of various countries in addition to providing wholesome physical activity and satis-fying mental and emotional experiences for all individuals immediately involved.

Folk dance is an excellent activity for sponsorship by schools or recreation centers in which entire families and community groups comprised of individuals from all walks of life may engage with wholesome satisfaction. When the Folk Festival Council, including various ethnological groups in the city of New York, first presented public programs in the Guild Theater for which paid admissions were in great demand, the leaders of this organization felt that one of the most salutary outcomes of the project was a closer knitting together of families comprised of children born in this country of parents and grandparents born and reared in the various countries from which they had migrated. In other words, these American-born children substituted a new respect for the dances, songs, and customs of their foreign-born parents for a somewhat condescending or embarrassed attitude when they found seasoned theater-goers in New York eager to pay for the privilege of seeing folk festivals of other lands re-enacted with all of their richness of color, costume, and tradition. Folk dance leaders in all parts of the country have observed that this particular activity has served as a means of bringing estranged members of individual American families together as well as those com-prising the more or less superficial socio-economic strata of various community groups.

NEUROMUSCULAR VALUES

The neuromuscular values of folk dance have to do with its inherent motor skills. Very often these neuromuscular skills are regarded as ends in themselves with too much emphasis placed upon their perfection. Prolonged emphasis upon the neuromuscular skills of folk dance may lead to self-consciousness and to fatigue, resulting in a subsequent distaste for this particular activity. They should be regarded primarily, therefore, as a *means* only to the larger goals established in terms of cultural, social and recreational values. Individuals, on the other hand, must be fairly skillful to enjoy folk dance and, unless they enjoy it, we know from the so-called laws of learning that they will not be likely to repeat the activity of their own volition. A continued, wholehearted experience in folk dance is prerequisite to the ulti-mate attainment of its broad, over-all aims.

The neuromuscular skills developed through folk dance are the basic or fundamental steps and figures which include the walk, run, skip, slide, jump, two-step, waltz in all its variations, various types of polka, schottische, step-hop, jig, and buzz steps common to the folk dances of many countries as well as those steps and figures which are peculiar to a specific country. Since all forms of dance were derived ultimately from folk dance, the neuromuscular skills developed in this particular activity afford a natural carry-over into the skillful performance of other types of dance including modern, ballroom, and tap. This is true not only with respect to dance in education but also with respect to dance in the theater. Such Broadway successes as *Brigadoon* and *Finian's Rainbow*, based respectively upon Scottish and Irish themes, not only utilize indigenous folk dances of these two countries but also reflect their influences in modern dance developed in theatrical idiom. Many of the basic folk dance steps are common to all dance forms as well as the same fundamentals of musical accompaniment — rhythm, accent, dynamics, quality of expression, and melodic line.

SPECIFIC OBJECTIVES

These foregoing values inherent in folk dance as an educational and recreational activity may be re-stated in the form of specific objectives with respect to knowledges to be acquired, skills to be mastered, and attitudes and appreciations to be developed. These objectives are stated in general terms to include all ages and educational levels of individuals who participate in folk dance. They should be adapted, therefore, to the needs and interests of each particular group and to the specific projects or classes in which the students are enrolled.

KNOWLEDGES TO BE ACQUIRED

1. To know the fundamental movements of which basic folk dance steps are made.
2. To know the sequence of fundamental movements, the rhythmic pattern, the dynamic pattern, and the space pattern for each specific folk dance step presented (e.g., step-hop, skip, schottische, waltz, polka, mazurka, varsovienne, two-step, *et cetera*).
3. To understand the use of rhythm, tempo, meter, phrasing, dynamics, and accent in the performance of folk dances.
4. To know the various countries from which specific folk dances come.
5. To know the origins of folk dances as they have developed in specific folk cultures.
6. To know the place of folk dance in the history of dance in general.
7. To know the relationship of dances from one country to those from other countries.
8. To understand the relationship of the folk dances of a specific country to the geographical, historical, and sociological background of that country.
9. To become acquainted with collections of folk dances and with literature related to folk dance.
10. To learn folk songs from the countries of the world.
11. To acquire information regarding the history of folk music and its influence upon music as a fine art.

12. To know the instruments which are used in accompanying folk dance and folk songs of various countries.
13. To learn about folk arts and crafts and the influence of folk arts upon painting and sculpture as fine arts.
14. To learn folk legends from all countries and to become aware of similarities in themes as they appear in the legends of various countries.
15. To know the influence of folk legends upon the themes and styles of expression in literature as a fine art.
16. To acquire information regarding folk costumes and the relationship of costume to the lives of the peoples involved.
17. To gather information about folk festivals as an expression of the life of the people of a particular time and place.
18. To know of leading personalities in the field of folk dance, including collectors of folk dances, directors of folk dancing, individuals who sponsor folk dance, and organizations devoted to the furtherance of folk dance.

Skills to be Mastered

1. To develop the ability to dance rhythmically with a poised, well-coordinated body which moves as one unit.
2. To perform step patterns accurately so that all hops, stamps, jumps, leaps, walking, and running steps are definite and accurately timed.
3. To dance accurately all accents in step patterns.
4. To describe a clean-cut, accurate floor pattern while dancing.
5. To dance forward, backward, sideward, and turning movements so that they are definite and properly spaced.
6. To dance all folk dance steps performed in combinations as phrases of movement rather than from step to step.
7. To dance all transitions from step to step and from figure to figure in a folk dance smoothly and easily so that there is no break in the movement of the dance from start to finish.
8. To develop a range of body movement in terms of flexibility and quality which is adequate and controlled in terms of the specific skills involved.
9. To execute each specific dance with appropriate style of body alignment.
10. To re-create accurately and effectively in the performance of every dance the spirit of the specific dance.

Attitudes and Appreciations to be Developed

1. To find satisfaction in the performance of solo folk dances.
2. To enjoy the fellowship and oneness of spirit which comes from participation in group folk dances.

31

3. To experience desirable attitudes toward practice and the perfection of performance in folk dances.
4. To appreciate skill in folk dance which is appropriate in style and spirit for each specific dance.
5. To appreciate the importance of good performance in folk dance as it influences one's own satisfaction and the satisfaction of those with whom one participates in folk dance experiences.
6. To feel a sense of responsibility conducive to reliability as a dancer in all group dances in the interest of safety and in the interest of the maintenance of integrity of the dance as a whole.
7. To develop an attitude of cooperation as a member of a group in folk dance.
8. To appreciate the contribution of folk peoples to the culture of the world.
9. To appreciate the contribution of the various ethnocentric groups in the United States to the heritage of this country.
10. To appreciate the value of folk dance as an activity for promoting understanding among the peoples of the world.

In addition to its cultural, social and recreational and neuromuscular values, folk dance is an activity, also, with certain administrative advantages in the conduct of an all-round physical education or recreation program. It requires no special equipment other than a smooth, level surface; it may be conducted either indoors or out. While a good accompanist and a piano simplify the teaching of folk dance, they are not indispensable to its presentation in that a number of folk dances have words that may be sung by the participants who thus provide their own means of accompaniment. Many folk dances are recorded — facilitating the use of a victrola or record player — and musical instruments such as the violin, accordion, banjo, and guitar are highly suitable for purposes of folk dance accompaniment since they were among the first instruments used for this purpose.

Folk dance is an activity which permits large classes or recreational groups since the skills involved are not so intricate as to demand a great deal of individualized instruction. It requires no special type of costume for general participation other than comfortable, low-heeled shoes and a costume which permits freedom of movement. It is an activity which is obviously and therefore admirably adapted to coeducational classes and corecreational groups with values accruing from such experiences; on the other hand, it is an activity also adapted to groups of the same sex where the situation does not permit mixed groups in that many folk dances are danced traditionally by men or by women only. Folk dance is also an excellent introduction to a broader rhythmic program for boys and men in that it is a form of dance traditionally associated with them and, therefore, not characterized by effeminacy in their regard.

Folk dance serves as an excellent opening wedge to a rhythmic program in a community that will not accept dance as such due to traditional taboos precluding participation in ballroom and other forms of dance through erroneous but none the less prejudicial associations. In this regard, communities may be re-educated gradually to accept dance as a wholesome form of recreation if parents participate first in folk dance, in much the same manner in which our ancestors in this country devised play-party games to avoid the term *dance* and the use of musical instruments for their accompaniment. In those communities in which a prejudice against dance prevails, a similar compromise in terminology might be advisable at first, such as substituting the term *rhythmics* for *dance* until the prejudices against dance as such are eradicated.

Chapter 3
Specific Methods in the Teaching of Folk Dance

The scene is a high school gymnasium of former years; unfortunately however, it is a scene which still obtains in many situations today. The participants are an instructor, a pianist, and a group of high school girls. The time is a physical education period. The instructor breaks the silence following roll call with, "All right, girls, number off in three's." Heads turn sharply from left to right as voices, in the rhythmic cadence of varying inflections, call out their respective numbers. The instructor continues, "Each set of three girls join hands in a circle. We are going to learn a dance called *The Crested Hen.* Take eight step-hops clockwise and eight counterclockwise. Let's try it with the music. All ready — go!"

And the girls go! Mechanically they dance through the A part, then the B, each outside girl skipping, in turn, under the arches formed by the other two. Presented thus as an exercise, this particular folk dance has failed to catch their imagination, to hold their interest, to satisfy any needs other than purely physiological ones of increased circulation and respiration that any equally vigorous activity might have satisfied quite as well. Furthermore, the girls are not particularly interested in having their respiration increased. Needless to say, they will not return to the dancing of *The Crested Hen* with any degree of pleasure; in fact, they may avoid all folk dancing as much as possible in the future.

THE CREATIVE APPROACH

In recent years, increasing emphasis has been placed upon the creative values of all educational activities. A necessity for the creative-values approach to curricular experiences is the logical outcome of an increasingly mechanized society in which innumerable labor-saving devices minimize the potentialities for creative effort on the part of those who employ them. At the same time, these devices curtail the outlets which, at one time, introduced essential satisfactions into the lives of men, women, and children everywhere. Not to dispense with fractionized labor on the assembly plan for speeding up production but to provide recreational activities—rich in creative values—during well-merited leisure hours is one of the basic goals of our modern plan of education for better living. Folk dance has inestimable potentialities for the implementation of such a plan.

Because folk dance is a traditional type of rhythmic activity, however, its steps and patterns necessarily shaped by preceding generations, teachers have been prone to ignore the creative experiences inherent in this phase of the educational curriculum. They have tended to think of creativeness in terms of improvisation only. Since "making up" a folk dance is obviously impossible, folk dances have been presented very often in a sterile, stereotyped manner of cut-and-dried steps and figures, punctiliously counted out and executed.

35

According to modern educational philosophy, no activity in which the student *really* participates is an old and decadent activity, devoid of creative implications. The old elements plus the new elements introduced by student participation result in something that *is* new — that the individual himself has created. Teachers of folk dance must be aware of the possibilities of this creative approach in folk dance. It is destroyed if dances are presented in the manner of the teacher described in her presentation of *The Crested Hen*. The creative approach is achieved when folk dances are presented in conjunction with their rich backgrounds of knowledges and appreciations and when ample opportunities are provided for real student participation in the exploration of these backgrounds. Obviously, the method of presentation will vary with the group according to their specific needs and interests. For example, at times the play elements in certain folk dances will be paramount; at other times, the ceremonial element will be emphasized; wherever pantomime and individual improvisation are indicated, these elements will be given free scope. The approach always, however, should be concerned with folk dance as a folk art.

The sound method of presenting folk dance as a creative activity differs from the one in the gymnasium scene described in that the teacher begins by giving students the atmosphere of the dance itself — i. e., *The Crested Hen*. He explains that the purpose of the dance is primarily social, performed by a man and two women. The dance to be taught comes from Denmark, a country in the northern part of Europe on the coast of the Baltic Sea, closely related in culture to Norway and Sweden, her Scandinavian cousins across the sea. The climate is cold in winter and warm in summer with frequent mists and rains because of Denmark's proximity to the sea. Agriculture and fishing are the chief industries. The peoples of Northern Europe, especially the Vikings from whom the Danes are descended, are a sturdy, spirited folk — hence, the vigorous style of many of their folk dances including *The Crested Hen* which derives its name from the fact that each woman as she skips under the joined hands of the man and the other woman in each set of three tries, in turn, to snatch the red stocking-cap from the head of the man and place it on her own — thus becoming a "crested hen." The basic step, a Danish skip or step-hop, is a vigorous, light one with strong elevation accented at the beginning of various phrases with a good stamp or a jump from both feet.

Through intelligent listening to music, the students are able to recognize that the mood of the accompaniment for *The Crested Hen* is gay and bright and that the quality of the music is overt, straightforward, and simple and suggests vigorous, spirited movement. They listen also to the structure of the music in terms of the contrasting parts or themes which give the dance a two-part form and in terms of the various phrases which make up each of these two parts. They listen for the basic underlying beat of the music which establishes its meter and for the accents which initiate each new phrase of music. While listening to the music they distinguish the basic step of the dance, the Danish skip or step-hop, as it is suggested by the rhythm of the music. With the type of presentation of a folk dance as outlined for *The Crested Hen*, the students learn more than a sequence of steps and their interest is stimulated with respect to the study of geography, history, and music as well as of folk dance—an interest which may prove enriching as it is extended into various interrelated areas.

If a specific dance involves difficult basic steps, the teacher may have the students clap the rhythm of the step with the music and practice the step at a slower tempo but always in the correct timing. He also preserves the continuity of learning basic skills by pointing out, wherever possible, the fact that new steps are made of combinations of simpler steps already learned. For the most part, the whole-part method of teaching folk dances should be used,[1] giving an overview first and then going back to improve individual and group performance rather than breaking the dance into parts to perfect positions and steps and then carrying other parts of the dance over into the next class period. With some of the longer, more difficult folk dances, this use of the so-called whole-part method is not always feasible; but with the shorter dances, it is both desirable and efficacious.

INTEGRATION AND CORRELATION

Some may question the creative approach to the teaching of folk dance by saying, "But after all, physical education is a period of activity and if too much time is spent in talking about habits, customs, costumes, and history, there will be little time left for the dancing itself." True, but it is not necessary to spend every minute of the physical education period in physical activity. Needed moments of rest may be utilized with discussion of the dance presented and of its background. Also, this problem may be solved—particularly at elementary and secondary school levels—through the generally accepted channels of integration of the physical education program within the school curriculum as a whole. For example, folk dance in the average secondary school may be integrated with subject matter material covered in connection with literature, ancient and modern languages, music and history. Scott's *Ivanhoe*, Tennyson's *Gareth and Wynette*, and Goldsmith's *Vicar of Wakefield* will prove all the richer for the reading if this experience is accompanied by the dancing of a suitable gavotte or minuet in accordance with the actual allusions to such traditional dance forms which appear in the texts themselves. Thus in *The Vicar of Wakefield*, high school students discover that a country dance, either similar to or identical with the *Sir Roger de Coverly* — immediate antecedent of America's *Virginia Reel* — was danced when Sophia and Olivia met the elegant town ladies who spoke glibly of "musical glasses" and referred, after dancing, to being "all of a muck of sweat." The potentialities for the integration of folk dance with other related subjects in the school curriculum are almost too obvious for comment.

The authors of *The Folk Dance Library* have had the satisfaction of presenting units of traditional dances in conjunction with state and regional conferences of teachers of English literature and various modern languages, thus establishing a pattern for the desirable integration of folk arts with the teaching of these subject matter areas in curriculums at all educational levels. Lecture-demonstrations pertinent to the history and development of folk song and dance in relation to the study of any given language, culminating in the general singing and dancing of simple but significant selections from these areas of the folk arts, will

---

[1]Hilda Chute Kozman, Rosalind Cassidy, and Chester O. Jackson, *Methods in Physical Education* (Philadelphia: W. B. Saunders Company, 1947), pp. 84, 386.

Jesse Feiring Williams, John I. Dambach, and Norma Schwendener, *Methods in Physical Education* (Philadelphia: W. B. Saunders Company, 1937), p. 43.

prove an invaluable medium for integrating activities too often confined to gymnasium and academic classrooms, respectively. The history of drama and of music are so inextricably linked with that of dance that a study of these three arts in any educational institution can ill afford to become disassociated if teachers are both well-informed and sincere in their guidance of students under their respective tutelage.

A single word of caution is apropos of this discussion of correlating the teaching of folk dance with that of other subject matter areas in the curriculum because it hinges upon an error so often committed in this regard. Instructors participating in an integrated program should avoid a fairly universal mistake by remembering that correlation does not mean the mere repetition of facts learned elsewhere or the duplication only of various educational experiences; rather, it implies the addition of new facts or points of view within the given areas of experience and the making of these facts more meaningful and significant through their relation to folk dance.

UNIT PLAN OF ORGANIZATION

Folk dance lends itself admirably to presentation in the unit or area plan of organization; such units may encompass the folk dances of a specific country, a race, or a period of civilization. For example, if an instructor wishes to present a unit of dances from the British Isles to a group of students, he should precede the actual presentation with a discussion of the geographical background of the countries involved, attempting to bring out as much of the information from the students as they recall from their previous study of geography or may integrate with such contemporary study. This background should include a view of a map so that the students may readily perceive the proximity of these countries to each other and to surrounding countries as well as their location in northern latitudes. The teacher should be prepared to supplement the students' contributions in terms of various industries of England, Scotland, and Ireland, varieties of terrain and climate. With the students thus oriented to the geographical features of the British Isles, a similar discussion should follow with reference to the historical and sociological backgrounds of the countries involved with emphasis upon their racial origins, early ancestry, relationships between each other throughout history in terms of conflicts and treaties of peace as well as the significant influences of neighboring countries. Such discussions as these do not require lengthy, detailed study of the history of the countries but should insure a sufficient background of the peoples so that the students of folk dance feel well enough acquainted with them to appreciate the various factors operative in the development of their respective dances.

A brief orientation to the characteristic types of folk dances from the British Isles should be presented in terms of general types and styles of movement, basic step patterns, formations, themes, *et cetera*. Bulletin boards should feature, at the time of a specific unit, a map of the countries, reproductions of authentic costumes, and pictures of landscapes as well as the actual display of authentic costumes and examples of various folk arts shown to advantage in a showcase. Throughout the presentation and performance of the folk dances of the British Isles, which may progress from simple through more difficult dances within the course of a specific unit, a general feeling of the color and life of the people should pervade the experience so that the students look upon the dances learned as the particularly beloved possessions of other folk like themselves which they, as students of folk dance, are privileged to share.

If a particular period in civilization is the basis of study, then the teacher is in a strategic position to show through one or more lecture-demonstrations — and through leadership in general participation — the dances engaged in for the given times and places studied, keying his presentations always into the *why* as well as the *how* of the particular folk dances illustrative of the specific era. For example, if students are studying the Middle Ages as a period of civilization, they may be taught a varied group of occupational folk dances in conjunction with their study of the period in history when Trade Guilds first flourished and developed such dances as a part of their identification with specific occupations or trades.

SPECIAL PROJECTS

Any number of special projects, pursued by individuals, or by groups of individuals comprising small committees, may prove invaluable media for the enrichment of the study of folk dance in the school or college curriculum. These special projects may be assigned definitely as extra-class requirements to supplement the regular class work and to serve as partial bases for the final awarding of marks or grades in accredited courses in folk dance, or they may be suggested and motivated as hobbies for individuals whose imaginations are genuinely kindled to further study in this area of the folk dance program.

These special projects may take any one of the following suggestive forms:

1. The collection of illustrations and data concerning folk costumes, folk festivals, folk arts, folk music — both songs and instruments for accompaniment — and other background materials.
2. The collection of dolls — either purchased or made and dressed at home — in authentic folk costumes.
3. The collection of folk legends.
4. The development of a character dance or study in folk dance idiom.
5. The presentation of a folk dance not taught in class but learned from a published collection of folk dances or from an authentic folk group in the locality of a specific school or college.

If properly directed and motivated, students may gain much that is enriching from keeping a scrapbook of interesting data and illustrations which they themselves gather through reading and conversation with others about the folk dances of various countries which they experience. Such a scrapbook might include their own summaries of pertinent information as well as articles and photographs gleaned from books, magazines and newspapers relative to the geography, history, costumes, festivals, legends, arts, crafts, and music of various folk groups. For clipping and pasting purposes, old copies of such magazines as *The National Geographic, Travel,* and *Holiday* may be purchased through bookstores and stands specializing in the back issues of these and similar publications. The holdings of any well-equipped school or college library afford copious reading and digesting of a wealth of information conducive to a creative and absorbing study of the folk dances of all nations.

Collections of small dolls dressed in authentic folk costumes may prove the beginning of an absorbing hobby. The dolls may be carved of wood by the student himself or purchased from the toy department of any store and dressed in traditional costumes representative of those worn by both men and women in various countries. The doll collection, on the other hand, may be accumulated through a careful selection and purchase of such figures in native dress from any number of reliable and authentic sources, especially those in large cities affording gift shops or special districts in which Americans from other lands are concentrated. Periodically, students should have the opportunity to exhibit their growing collections.

The development of a character dance or a study in folk dance idiom is particularly challenging as a creative experience after students have become thoroughly acquainted with a number of folk dances from any given country. Well imbued with the style, characteristic steps, and formations of typical dances of the specific country, students might be encouraged to seek suitable folk songs for which recorded folk dances are not available, and to develop folk dance studies in keeping with the form of the songs selected. This project should be assigned with the particular caution that the resulting experience is, to be sure, *not* a folk dance in the traditional sense but a *character dance* or a *folk dance study* with its opportunities to test creative abilities in fitting suitable steps to appropriate folk music and in preserving the forms established by the latter. In making such an assignment, the stipulation of using folk songs to which there are no recorded dances at the present time will further obviate any confusion which might arise regarding the distinction between genuine folk dances and deliberately created folk dance studies or character dances in folk dance idiom.

The presentation of a folk dance either learned from an ethnological source within the community or from a published collection of authentic folk dances is particularly important for professional preparation courses designed to fuse methods of teaching with materials for those being trained as potential leaders in this area of the educational curriculum. These students should not only become acquainted with the available literature in the form of recorded, authentic folk dances and well-versed in their abilities to interpret correctly and to transmit directions recorded by authorities in this field, but should be encouraged also to seek out those individuals and groups in their respective communities who have brought to their present localities rich heritages of folklore from other lands. Mary Effie Shambaugh, in her quest for authentic folk dance materials in various foreign countries, was told again and again by villagers in these countries that "the man who really knows the most about our folk dances now lives in 'such-and-such' a city in the United States of America." Her plea that we explore the resources within our immediate reach has proved a sound one, and many a class in folk dance under the immediate supervision of the authors of *The Folk Dance Library* has been enriched immeasurably by having individuals and groups of a specific locality teach and demonstrate, in native costumes, the dances which they have brought and preserved from the homelands from which they migrated.

Any academic assignment — whether in the form of scrapbooks or doll collections — runs the risk of becoming meaningless "busy work" unless properly motivated and resulting from a genuine interest on the part of those who undertake it. Academic assignments, as such, are sometimes questionable in connection with required courses in folk dance at secondary school or college level when primary objectives should be directed toward the development of skill in performance with such a genuine love of the activity that the skill will be pursued at every opportunity for achievement of the social and recreational objectives previously outlined. Wherever academic assignments become a chore without the proper motivation of genuine interest to pursue them, they may mitigate against the achievement of a sincere love for and subsequent participation in folk dance as a rich, leisure-time pursuit. A wise teacher, therefore, will be cognizant of the pitfalls and will guide students enrolled in such classes to achieve the cultural-interest objectives outlined, tempering his academic requirements accordingly.

Particularly to be deplored is the more or less universal practice of requiring major students in health, physical education, and recreation to keep notebooks which, in the final analysis, result in little beyond the copying of music and directions for folk dances presented in conjunction with their professional preparation as potential leaders in this field. Their time outside of class should be spent to better advantage in the pursuit of any one of the several projects described and they should thus be encouraged to acquire, in a legitimate fashion, a professional library made possible by those who have devoted endless hours of time, study, and energy to the folk dance collections available for their use. To supplement, but not to duplicate, these materials should be a basic objective of every folk dance course in teacher-education institutions.

CULMINATING ACTIVITIES

Modern educational methodology stresses the importance of culminating activities for any given unit of study for the purpose of tying together or unifying the various learning experiences involved. In this connection, a particularly rich use of folk dance materials lies in the production of a festival in which the entire school or college community participates. These festivals may be built around any one of many possible themes. They may take the form of seasonal festivals based upon the harvest season, Christmas, spring, *et cetera*. A harvest festival may be of an indigenous nature, such as a Corn-Husking Bee similar to those held by our pioneer ancestors, or it may take the form of a re-enactment of the harvest celebrations observed in other countries. The same basic idea may serve as the nucleus for the celebration of other special holidays or seasons in keeping with the principles outlined for successful festival production in the present volume and based upon the specific festal occasions described as a part of each of the units presented in the remaining four volumes of *The Folk Dance Library*.

Another culminating project of folk dance classes may take the form of special parties. Thus a unit in Mexican folk dances may be climaxed with a Mexican folk dance party to which students come costumed and participate in Mexican folk dances as well as in other customs associated with this country with typical Mexican refreshments served in the course of the evening's program. Such a party might, of course, evolve from a study of English folk dances or from those of any other single country or region representative of a group of countries closely related in a geographical sense. In each instance, the pattern for the culminating project might follow the basic principles established for such activities and should prove an enriching experience in the study of folk dance at all educational levels.

Although it may seem entirely superfluous in any discussion of the methods of teaching folk dance, the authors feel the necessity of a final word of caution in the utilization of the materials included in *The Folk Dance Library*. Under no circumstances should any degree of license be employed with respect to the adaptation of the dances analyzed to any particular group or situation. In other words, every effort has been made to preserve their authenticity as to form, step patterns, sequence, and style. Any effort, therefore, to adapt particular dances to specific groups or purposes is decried. To lengthen or to shorten any given folk dance by adding or omitting the steps analyzed, or the "dressing up" of particular figures and formations through a desire to make them more spectacular is greatly deplored.

ACCOMPANIMENT

Accompaniment for folk dance activities was discussed briefly in conjunction with administrative advantages in a preceding section of the present volume. It is a topic of such importance in the opinions of the authors, however, as to merit further mention in this discussion of special methods in the field of folk dance.

Very often the accompaniment for folk dance classes in educational institutions is relegated to a high school or college student in substitution for her active participation in a required program of physical education. This is an unsound practice, not only from the viewpoint of the student herself, but also from the viewpoint of the activity for all involved since good accompaniment presupposes a skillful and sympathetic artist. Only an experienced accompanist — one preferably employed as a regular member of the educational or recreational staff — can provide the piano accompaniments for folk dances which contribute to their correct execution with respect to tempo, style, quality, *et cetera*.

In the piano arrangements presented for the accompaniment of the various folk dances analyzed in the remaining four volumes of *The Folk Dance Library*, every effort has been made to indicate correct tempi and qualities consonant with the proper execution of the various steps and figures constituting each folk dance presented. For example, a light, tinkling quality, redolent of traditional music boxes, should characterize the accompaniment for the Bavarian dances analyzed in *Folk Dances of European Countries*, and a humming, strumming, droning, quality, suggestive of the *binjou*, for the French dances in the same volume; in like fashion, a smooth, running quality of accompaniment is indicated for the English country dances in *Folk Dances of the British Isles*. Strict adherence to the tempi designated by the metronomic marks listed for each dance should obtain and the pianist should keep folk dance accompaniments simple, direct, and pure with respect to the particular quality and form indicated in each instance. Thus the pianist who contributes to the spirit and quality of a dance with a sensitive accompaniment finds the experience creative rather than one of monotonous routine.

Properly played, the piano accompaniments for folk dances may prove a real aid to students in learning the correct phrasing, accents, and dynamics of any given dance. Any elaboration, "jazzing," or other distortion of the musical settings for authentic folk dances is decried as well as a substitution of melodies other than those prescribed unless such substitution is permissible as in the case of specific folk dances of the United States included in *Folk Dances of the United States and Mexico.*

Wherever possible, the use of traditional instruments such as bagpipes, zithers, guitars, and violins, is desirable for the accompaniments of the folk dances analyzed in *The Folk Dance Library* as indicated in the overviews of dances in each unit. An ingenious teacher in the average community can find local musicians to visit folk dance classes occasionally so that students may have the experience of performing specific dances to the instruments traditionally associated with their performance,—an experience conducive to a better appreciation of the particular quality or qualities sought.

The use of singing accompaniments for many of the dances should be utilized fully for the additional satisfactions accruing from the exercise of vocal cords along with that of limbs. And finally, more and more folk dance melodies are being recorded by the larger record companies for the purpose of providing accompaniments for folk dances in situations affording the use of victrolas only as well as of insuring correct accompaniments with respect to tempi and quality for folk dances thus recorded. Such records are listed in the catalogues of various record companies.

Chapter 4
Folk Dance as a Coeducational and Corecreational Activity

Modern educators are becoming increasingly concerned with the problem of developing programs conducive to the integration of the individual graduated from any given educational level. Their interest in this regard has been aroused by the somewhat startling statistics with respect to the increase of juvenile delinquency, adult crime, divorces and broken homes, mental, nervous, and functional diseases, and all other concrete evidences of emotional maladjustments and failure to meet the problems of everyday living in an objective, straightforward, and socially approved fashion. Their concern is heightened further by the realization that, since World War II, this problem of social maladjustment has become more acute in the United States than at any previous time.

Primitive man and his descendants in folk peoples of simpler cultures than those which obtain in urban centers in all parts of the world today were completely integrated in that the various facets of their lives — work, play, worship, education, mating, and establishing homes — were fused in a single and logical pattern devoid of the frustrations and conflicts introduced by the complexities of achieving maturity and the taking of one's place in a highly mechanized society. To preclude the development and subsequent manifestations of these conflicts, educators have established integration of the individual and its correlative — personal adjustment to the prevailing mores of society — as a basic goal and are selecting those experiences deemed most conducive to its achievement as the core of educational curriculums today. Toward this end, a well-conducted program of folk dance is one of the activities highly recommended.

Psychologists tell us that the process of adjustment to one's place as an adult in the modern world entails two basic steps. The first is concerned with breaking away from one's family in the sense of developing one's own individuality and of establishing a sort of psychological independence. The second is the development of a normal interest in the opposite sex. Most of the emotional problems of the adult are associated with the degree to which these two basic steps in adjustment are made successfully.

Surely folk dance is one of the most expedient media for effecting these two psychological goals. Essentially a social activity, it promotes a wholesome sort of companionship between boys and girls with attention somewhat focused, at the same time, upon an objective, expressive skill. The development of folk dance skills contributes to a sense of assurance and well-being with a subsequent ease of adjustment in mixed social groups. Not only may sex consciousness be minimized, but also many appreciations and understanding of the opposite sex may be engendered. By contributing to the development of a normal degree of heterosexuality, folk dance is, at the same time, conducive to a psychological sort of weaning from family ties

45

since the two adjustments are related in a subtle but very real fashion. Paradoxical as it may seem, folk dance may also prove an invaluable medium for cementing family ties that are not constricting to the psychological independence of offspring because it means the wholesome sharing of a mutual, innate interest. Thus the parents in families of folk peoples everywhere have handed down to their children the folk dances constituting their familial and racial heritage, taking it for granted that skill in their performance should be effected as a result of participation beginning in early childhood and continuing into adulthood when children leave parental homes to establish those of their own making and, in turn, perpetuate the patterns indigenous to their respective cultures.

The question of coeducation in the United States — and of its sequel, corecreation — is an exceedingly interesting one in view of the historical background from which it has developed. The problem in the beginning of organized instruction was not one of a *segregation* of the sexes for educational purposes. It was, instead, a question of the *selection* of the male sex only as being worthy of educational advantages. The grammar schools of the seventeenth and eighteenth centuries in this country, therefore, were founded for boys alone.

Calling names is a futile practice and, in this case, we cannot isolate too specifically those who should be denounced for responsibility in thus stigmatizing the feminine sex. Regardless of who was first responsible for woman's lowly status in the educational world, various religious and economic factors had some weight in maintaining this status for many years. Looked upon as the chattel or property of the so-called stronger sex, there was no need for the formal education of women in the same sense in which men were thought to need such instruction.

Within a span of years, however, the question arose as to whether women should be offered educational advantages. This was a subject of heated controversy during the early part of the nineteenth century. When the matter of public schools and academies for girls came up for discussion in town meetings, speakers arose to argue two sides of the question. There were invariably those who maintained that women were not fit for education, and there were those who maintained just as staunchly that education was not fit for women — that is, that it would prove degrading to their finer, feminine souls. Champions of both sides were benighted, to be sure, but women feel a little more sympathetic toward those who avouched the latter view.

Quite logically, then, the first formal education for women took place in academies for girls only. This was due to three main factors. The first was the prevailing concept of innate differences between the natures of boys and girls calling for different kinds of educational environment. It was the same sort of notion which prompted such nursery rhymes as

> *What are little boys made of, made of,*
> *What are little boys made of?*
> *Snips and snails, and puppy-dogs' tails;*
> *And that's what little boys are made of, made of.*

What are little girls made of, made of,
What are little girls made of?
Sugar and spice, and all that's nice;
And that's what little girls are made of, made of.

The second factor responsible for the segregative education of boys and girls is that women, in those days, were not supposed to speak publicly in the presence of men. Hence, they could not recite in mixed groups. And finally, separate schools were in keeping with the markedly different type of education to which the two sexes were exposed. Since woman's only vocation was marriage, her education was concerned primarily with matters of homemaking.

A coeducational high school was opened in Providence, Rhode Island, as early as 1843. After that time, new schools were founded for both sexes, and the coeducation of boys and girls became a well-established practice. In time, physical education was added to the school curriculum. In the upper elementary grades and junior high schools, special teachers were employed — a man for the boys, a woman for the girls — and the two sexes were again separated for their activities in this particular field. The separation of the sexes was based upon the assumption of certain anatomical and physiological differences necessitating a different kind of physical education. While the assumption was sound with respect to a few activities in physical education, it was unsound in that it resulted in the extreme practice of separating boys and girls for *all* physical education activities.

Granted, then, that boys and girls should be separated for some of their instruction, what criteria can we establish for determining those activities in which they should engage together? In the main, the authors suggest the criterion that those activities are suitable for coeducation in which the basic elements are *skill* rather than strength, *agility* rather than endurance, and freedom from bodily contact of a combative nature. A second criterion might be one of interest although it would seem that, apart from training and tradition, few activities which measure up to the first criterion would fail to interest both sexes.

If these criteria are accepted as bases for determining coeducational and corecreational activities in physical education, it is immediately recognized that folk dance should be taught to mixed classes wherever possible. Skill and agility are certainly its basic elements; the particular kind of endurance demanded is of a highly individual nature, subject to the control of the individual rather than to the pressure and time element of a team sport like basketball. There is no more reason, therefore, to separate boys and girls for classes in folk dance than there is to separate them for classes in history and English literature. In addition to satisfying the foregoing criteria for its suitability as a coeducational and corecreational activity in the field of physical education, folk dance may serve as a very significant medium for achieving the primary values of coeducation in any field of education.

While the majority of the dances analyzed in the various volumes of *The Folk Dance Library* are designed for participation on the part of mixed groups, the authors have included a number of dances performed traditionally by men or by women alone. Obviously, all of the folk dances presented are appropriate for inclusion in the materials for professional preparation of potential teachers and leaders in this branch of the folk arts. While it is preferable to have the couple dances performed only by mixed groups, the authors feel that there are educational benefits to be derived from their performance by groups of school girls or college women in those situations in which the participation of male partners is not possible. The same principle applies to the performance on the part of girls and women of folk dances traditionally associated with men only, such as the English Morris and sword dances. While their recommendation may seem inconsistent in this regard, they suggest that social, couple dances *not* be used for groups of boys or men alone except in teacher-education situations and then only after the possibilities for providing women partners have been fully explored without success.

Chapter 5
Evaluation of the Teaching of Folk Dance

As long as a program of folk dance is conducted solely for the purpose of recreation, the only necessary form of evaluation is in terms of the satisfactions· evinced by those participating. To be sure, these satisfactions are dependent in large measure upon the achievement of the same objectives sought when folk dance is taught as a definite part of the school curriculum; the successful leader, therefore, must direct his efforts toward their realization although he may forego the more academic evaluative procedures prerequisite to the awarding of marks or grades. Folk dance as a part of the regular, accredited program of physical education in the school or college curriculum, on the other hand, necessitates periodic evaluation of the progress of the students enrolled in such classes so that the teacher may have concrete evidence of the success with which he is guiding these students toward the realization of the goals established.

The outcomes sought, established by the instructor in collaboration with the students enrolled in his classes, are expressed usually in terms of knowledges to be acquired, skills to be mastered, and attitudes and appreciations to be developed. Knowledges to be acquired are those which pertain to information regarding the background of the folk dances of a specific unit including influences of a geographical, historical, and sociological nature which have resulted in the shaping of origins, themes, and styles of the folk dances of a given time and place as well as knowledges regarding the various factors of form, tempo, dynamics, rhythmic patterns, step patterns, style, accent, and quality which are involved in the performance of any specific folk dance. Skills to be mastered are concerned with the correct performance of particular dances and include the accurate execution of steps and the good performance of dances with respect to their appropriate style and quality. Attitudes and appreciations to be developed are those which relate to an appreciation of the contributions of various countries to a vital folk art which is shared by all peoples everywhere as well as to an appreciation of participation in dance as a significant area of human experience.

Unless objectives sought and listed are linked directly with some means of evaluation to ascertain the extent to which they are realized, the instructors in charge of accredited courses in folk dance in educational institutions at various levels are guilty of wishful thinking. It behooves them, therefore, to develop some means of evaluating the outcomes of their respective programs in this particular area of the curriculum in schools and colleges.

THE EVALUATION OF KNOWLEDGE OBJECTIVES

A basic principle of measurement prescribes that all outcomes to be evaluated should be considered in the light of objectives established as goals for a specific class. The teacher and the students are successful to the extent to which outcomes of their class experiences approximate the goals established. The following outline presents important factors included in knowledge objectives with suggestive criteria to be used in the evaluation of the students' achievement with respect to each of the specific factors listed.

1. Basic folk dance steps, positions, and formations.

   Knows the fundamental movements, that is, the walk, run, leap, hop, jump, stamp, *et cetera*, of which basic folk dance steps consist, and the sequence of these movements, the rhythmic pattern, the dynamic pattern, and the space pattern for each specific step. The number of basic folk dance steps to be known thus depends upon those which appear in dances learned but will probably include the step-hop, skip, schottische, waltz, polka, mazurka, varsovienne, two-step, *et cetera*.

   Knows the basic positions, including open and closed social dance positions, shoulder-waist position, open social dance position with partners side by side and inside hands joined at shoulder level, *et cetera*.

   Knows basic group formations, including a single circle with partners facing, all facing in, or with all facing clockwise or counterclockwise; a double circle with partners facing each other, or with partners side by side facing clockwise, or counterclockwise; a longways set with all facing up or with partners facing; a duple minor set both in circular and longways formations; a square or quadrille formation; *et cetera*.

2. Rhythm, tempo, meter, phrasing, pitch, dynamics, and accent.

   Understands the use of rhythm, tempo, meter, phrasing, pitch, dynamics, and accent in folk dance.

3. Origins of folk dance.

   Knows the origins of folk dances studied, knows the countries from which they come, knows the place of folk dance in the history of all forms of dance, and knows the relationship of dances studied from one country to those studied from other countries.

4. Relation of folk dance to the geographical, historical, and sociological backgrounds of a specific country or region.

   Understands the relationship between the folk dances of a specific country and the geographical, historical, and sociological backgrounds of that country, recognizing the influences which these factors have exercised in shaping the development of the dances themselves.

5. Folk dance literature.

   Is familiar with books or magazines in which folk dances are recorded and with literature pertaining to the history of folk dance.

6. Folklore—songs, legends, music, arts, festivals.

   Knows folk songs and legends from the various countries whose folk dances are studied.
   Knows the general characteristics of the folk music and folk arts from each of the countries studied and the development of these folk arts into the fine arts in various areas.
   Knows the major festivals of both sacred and secular origin in the countries studied and some details as to the nature of these celebrations.

7. Personalities in folk dance.

Knows the contributions of specific leaders in this area in terms of those who have contributed to folk dance literature, to the teaching or leadership of folk dance, and to its regular performance. Such information should include contemporary leaders as well as those of the past.

8. Organizations in the field of folk dance.

Knows the names of outstanding folk dance organizations and something of their respective programs in terms of regularly scheduled and special activities.

The extent to which specific knowledges are acquired may be ascertained readily by means of sound, objective, written examinations based upon any one or more of several standardized forms with questions phrased as true-false, multiple-choice, completion, and matching types generally established as means of evaluating information or knowledges pertaining to any subject in the curriculum. Letter grades which represent an evaluation of knowledge objectives may be secured by arranging the numerical scores made by students on such objective tests first into a frequency distribution and then translating these numerical scores into letter grades in accordance with any one of several approved statistical procedures.[1] Because the allocation of grades or marks is generally based upon the assumption of a normal curve of distribution, the teacher of folk dance should keep in mind two important factors that must obtain before the arbitrary allocation of a given percentage of each of the five traditional letter grades, or their categorization through a definite increment in terms of the standard deviation on either side of the mean as a measure of central tendency, is warranted. The arbitrary allocation of marks based upon a normal curve of distribution is feasible only when first, fairly large groups of students serve as subjects for the tests administered and second, when the group tested is unselected insofar as both information and skill in folk dance are concerned. In other words, the instructor of a somewhat small, advanced, or selected group of students in folk dance should expect relatively higher achievement scores in the measurement of both information and skill in this area of the school or college curriculum rather than scores which range over what is known as a normal curve of distribution, and should adjust accordingly his translation of such scores into marks or letter grades. In a group of any size, however, there may be a student whose score stands out from those of the other students either as very high or very low. These scores are termed "spurious" by statisticians and, while they are included in the frequency distribution, they are given special consideration in the determination of letter grades from the total distribution of such scores.

The objective examination which follows includes items which are illustrative of the various types of questions that may serve as a means of evaluating the items of information regarding folk dance listed under knowledge objectives. Some of the items included are difficult and some are simple; all of them cover materials included in *The Folk Dance Library*. Answers to the various items included should be scored according to the customary procedures

---

[1]Bases for determining letter marks which are used frequently include (1) quartiles, (2) percentiles, (3) standard deviations from the mean, and (4) normal breaks among the scores comprising the frequency distribution into which they are grouped.

for scoring objective examinations, i.e., the subtraction of the total number of items incorrectly answered from those correctly answered in the section of the examination based upon true or false statements, and the awarding of one point for each of the items correctly answered in those sections of the examination based upon multiple choice, completion, and matching types of objective examinations. Each part of the test should be scored separately, therefore, and the final score computed by adding the scores on each part of the objective examination.

Illustrative Objective Examination for the Evaluation of Knowledge Objectives

Letter Grade_____

Name_____   Score: Part I _____   Part IV   _____

Class_____ Date_____   Part II _____   Part V   _____

Part III_____   Total Score_____

PART I. The following statements are preceded by the letters *T* and *F*. Encircle the letter *T* if the statement is true. Encircle the letter *F* if the statement, or any part of the statement, is false. *Do not guess*. If you are unable to decide whether a statement is true or false, leave it alone. You will be penalized for each statement marked incorrectly by having one point deducted from the number of statements marked correctly.

Example: (T) F   We are indebted chiefly to Cecil Sharp for the collection of English folk dances.

T F 1. The characteristics of a people of a specific time and place can be discerned from a study of their folk dances.

T F 2. The spirit of a folk dance reflects the life of the people.

T F 3. There is one authentic way for executing each traditional folk dance.

T F 4. The same folk dances are known in all parts of a given country.

T F 5. The country in which the people manifest a keen sense of beauty invariably proves fertile soil for the rich development of folk dance.

T F 6. A national dance is a traditional dance of the given country.

T F 7. National dance and character dance are synonymous terms and may be used interchangeably.

T F 8. Folk dances which were once occupational in origin may have lost the characteristic pantomime which distinguishes them as such.

T F 9. Clog and shuffle steps, familiar to the peasant dances of many countries, reached the state of greatest elaboration and perfection among the Irish people.

T F 10. The United States of America does not have a national dance.

T F 11. Square dances are not performed in the New England states.

T F 12. There are eight standard American schottisches.

T F 13. American and English country dances, sharing a common origin, are similar in their style of execution.

T F 14. Whereas folk dance terminology differs widely in various countries, there is marked similarity between the terminology used in English and American country dances.

T F 15. English folk tunes are used as accompaniment for some of the American folk dances.

T F 16. The fact that English Morris and sword dances were danced originally by men alone gives them prestige upon the rhythmic program for boys and men.

T F 17. According to some authorities, the custom of Morris dancers of blackening their faces prior to their performance is linked with the derivation of the name "Morris" for this type of dance.

T F 18. While dances similar to the English Morris, sword, and country dances were known in other countries, they seem to have survived more generally in England than elsewhere.

T F 19. The English country dances were derived from the original May Day dances.

T F 20. The English country dances are social in origin and significance.

T F 21. Irish dances are like English dances in their freedom from affectation.

T F 22. The Scottish sword dances, like the English sword dances, are performed by groups with intricate team patterns.

T F 23. The rugged thriftiness and precision of the Scottish race is reflected in their dances.

T F 24. Danish dances lack variety as to theme.

T F 25. All Norwegian dances are vigorous and highly social in nature.

T F 26. Swedish dances are often rich in pantomime and story elements.

T F 27. The Swedish *Oxen Dance* is a dance of courtship.

T F 28. The Swedish *Dal Dance* has sociological implications as to the former status of women in that country.

T F 29. The Danish *Nixie Polka* is an occupational dance.

T F 30. The *Highland Fling* was originally a war dance performed on the eve of impending battles.

T F 31. The *Scottish Sword Dance* is illustrative of folk dances based upon the theme of war.

T F 32. The American *Virginia Reel* was derived directly from the Irish *Rinnce Fadha*.

T F 33. The Bavarian *Schuhplattler* can be traced back to the animal dances of a former period.

T F 34. The *Csárdás* is the national dance of Russia.

T F 35. The festivals known as the *Feis* played an important part in perpetuating the folk arts of the Irish people.

T F 36. The *Tarantella* is the national dance of Italy.

T F 37. The *Tarantella*, as it is danced in Italy, is a couple dance with a definite sequence of steps and figures.

T F 38. The *Jarabe Tapatío* is the national dance of Mexico.

T F 39. The "hey" is the introductory figure for English Morris dances.

T F 40. In "siding" in English country dances, partners pass by right shoulders, returning to place by left shoulders.

T F 41. "Arming" in English country dances is usually danced right, then left.

T F 42. "Turn single" in English country dances involves a clockwise turn.

T F 43. The term "floor pattern" indicates the design made on the floor by the path of the dancer during the course of a dance.

T F 44. The outside foot is the foot which is toward the outside of the circle when partners are standing in a double circle facing clockwise or counterclockwise.

T F 45. In open social dance position of partners in folk dance, the girl stands on the right of her partner.

T F 46. In closed social dance position, partners start the first step on the same foot.

T F 47. According to certain folk dance authorities, the polka step is so called because it was first danced by Polish women who were called *Polska*.

T F 48. Successive polka steps are begun on opposite feet.

T F 49. The polka step is a smooth, even step with a time signature in 4/4 meter.

T F 50. The waltz may be described thus: step L, step R, close L.

T F 51. A schottische is built upon the same rhythmic pattern as the polka.

T F 52. The schottische may be danced in different ways but must be performed to music in 3/4 meter.

T F 53. The simplest form of the schottische may be described thus: slide L, cut R, leap L, step R.

T F 54. The varsovienne is a dance form in 3/4 meter common to many countries.

T F 55. The traditional varsovienne is a combination of the waltz, the mazurka, and the schottische.

T F 56. Step-hops and skips both have uneven rhythmic patterns.

T F 57. The Danish skip is in reality a step-hop.

T F 58. In dancing continuous step-hops, the body weight remains on the right foot.

T F 59. In a two-step, the feet are in closed position on the second step.

T F 60. Successive mazurka steps are begun on the same foot.

T F 61. A single buzz step permits the dancer to cover little distance.

T F 62. The gavotte arose in Spain but was perfected in France.

T F 63. Dance forms like the gavotte and minuet became the settings for musical compositions.

T F 64. Gavottes and minuets are confined to the folk dances of France.

T F 65. Increasing the tempo means decreasing the speed of the music or dance.

T F 66. A phrase is a unit of music structure which is complete in itself.

T F 67. A series of phrases are used to build a measure of music.

T F 68. In folk dance, music should be utilized for purposes of accompaniment only.

T F 69. An original dance composition which is composed to folk music and which uses characteristic folk dance steps and formations should be called a folk dance study.

T F 70. Although folk dances are necessarily "ready made" material, the teaching of folk dance may prove a creative experience for students.

T F 71. Enough skill to enjoy folk dance is essential if objectives other than physiological ones are to be achieved.

T F 72. Mary Wood Hinman and Elizabeth Burchenal stand out for their contributions to the folk dance movement both for their collection of materials and for their services to organizations dedicated to the furtherance of folk dance and its related arts.

T F 73. The Folk Festival Council was an organization comprised of various ethnological groups in New York.

T F 74. May Gadd is the leader of the American Folk Dance Society.

T F 75. Gomme, Newell, Vuillier, Sharp, Oppé, and the Kinneys offer sources of information through which we may enrich our backgrounds for the teaching of folk dance.

PART II. Each of the statements below is followed by several alternative phrases or words. Select the one phrase or word which makes the statement complete and true. Underscore your choice and write the number of the phrase or word in the space provided in the column on the right of each item. You will receive one point for each item answered correctly.

Example: The man who first recorded and published a collection of English country dances was (1) Sharp (2) Arbeau (3) Byrd (4) Playford.   __4__

1. Tempo refers to (1) rate of speed, (2) time beat, (3) dynamics, (4) phrasing.   _____

2. In American country dance, round dances are those (1) danced in a circle formed by any number of dancers, (2) danced in couples independent of other couples, (3) danced in a circle formed by twelve dancers, (4) in which couples revolve continuously while dancing.   _____

3. The polka may be described as (1) hop L, step R, step L, close R, (2) step R, step L, close R, hop R, (3) step L, close R, hop R, step L, (4) hop L, step R, close L, step R.   _____

4. The polka is said to have originated in (1) Poland, (2) France, (3) Bohemia, (4) Bulgaria.   _____

5. The waltz originated in (1) France, (2) Italy, (3) Germany, (4) Poland.   _____

6. The slide has the same step pattern as the (1) skip, (2) gallop, (3) step-hop, (4) two-step. _____

7. The *ländler* is an early dance form from which evolved the (1) mazurka, (2) polka, (3) waltz, (4) two-step. _____

8. The "rose" as a folk dance figure is associated with (1) American country dances, (2) English sword dances, (3) French court dances, (4) the Italian national dance. _____

9. A Mexican dance usually performed on a wooden platform which derives its name from Aztec words meaning "a place covered with wood" is the (1) *jarabe*, (2) *jarana*, (3) *huapango*, (4) *zapateado*. _____

10. Those dances of France which developed into highly artificial and polished court dances had their origin among (1) the people of the court, (2) the peasant folk of the country, (3) slaves brought from conquered countries, (4) groups of traveling dancers. _____

11. The Celtic ancestors of the English people migrated to the British Isles from (1) the continent of Europe, (2) the Scandinavian Peninsula, (3) Iceland, (4) the Iberian Peninsula. _____

12. The official languages of Switzerland are (1) German and French, (2) German, French, and Italian, (3) German, French, and Swiss, (4) German, French, Italian, and Romansh. _____

13. The largest Scandinavian country — in terms of area of land — is (1) Norway, (2) Sweden, (3) Finland, (4) Denmark. _____

14. The most elaborately and widely celebrated seasonal festival in Scandinavia is (1) New Year's Day, (2) Christmas Day, (3) Midsummer Eve, (4) Easter. _____

15. The patron saint of Mexico is (1) St. James, (2) *La Virgen de Guadalupe*, (3) *El Santo Señor de Chalma*, (4) St. Joseph. _____

16. The *langeleik* is a musical instrument first used to accompany folk dances in (1) Denmark, (2) Finland, (3) Norway, (4) Sweden. _____

17. *Edelweiss* is a (1) flower found high in the Alps, (2) favorite beverage of the Swiss people, (3) portion of the costume worn by Bavarian men, (4) festal food enjoyed at the Christmas season in Germany. _____

18. The *sporran* is (1) a purse worn as a part of the Scottish Highlander's costume, (2) a dark shawl worn by Irish women in that country, (3) a kind of suspender worn by a Morris dancer, (4) the scarf worn over the shoulder by the Scottish Highlander. _____

19. The *piñata* is a (1) large woolen blanket worn as a cloak by Mexican men, (2) pilgrimage made by Mexican people to a religious shrine, (3) container made in the image of a fowl or animal which is filled with "goodies" and broken during festivities in Mexico, (4) play commemorating the flight of the Holy Family to Bethlehem which is produced each Christmas in Mexico. _____

PART III. Place in the *blank space* before each of the items in the column on the left the *number* of the item in the column on the right which best matches it. You will receive one point for each blank space filled with the correct number.

1. *Fundamental steps and terms:*

_ _ _ _ _ Both feet leave the floor at the same time.

_ _ _ _ _ Feet are brought together.

_ _ _ _ _ Performed on one foot; may be repeated on same foot.

_ _ _ _ _ Dancer leaves the floor as weight is changed to opposite foot.

_ _ _ _ _ Weight changed from one foot to the other; dancer always retains contact with floor.

1. Hop
2. Skip
3. Close
4. Leap
5. Jump
6. Walk

2. *Dance positions and directions:*

_ _ _ _ _ Dancer standing on left of partner.

_ _ _ _ _ Dancer standing on right of partner.

_ _ _ _ _ Partners face in opposite directions.

_ _ _ _ _ Facing in, dancers move left in a circle.

_ _ _ _ _ Facing in, dancers move right in a circle.

1. Woman's position in open social dance position
2. Man's position in open social dance position
3. Left-hand mill position
4. Clockwise direction
5. Counterclockwise direction
6. Right-hand mill position
7. Closed social dance position

3. *Step analyses:*

_ _ _ _ _ Run, run, run, hop.

_ _ _ _ _ Hop, step, close, step.

_ _ _ _ _ Step, hop (even rhythm).

_ _ _ _ _ Step, hop (uneven rhythm).

_ _ _ _ _ Step, close, step.

_ _ _ _ _ Step, step, close.

1. Waltz
2. Polka
3. Schottische
4. Skip
5. Step-hop
6. Slide
7. Run
8. Two-step

57

4. *Authors and titles of books pertaining to folk dance:*

_ _ _ _ _ *Folk Dances of Germany*   1. Curt Sachs

                                             2. Elizabeth Burchenal

_ _ _ _ _ *The Book of Days*   3. Lincoln Kirstein

                                               4. Gaston Vuillier

_ _ _ _ _ *Swedish Folk Dances*   5. Kathleen Mann

                                               6. Nils Bergquist

_ _ _ _ _ *Pre-Classic Dance Forms*   7. Ethel Urlin

                                               8. Louis Horst

_ _ _ _ _ *The Dance; Its Place in Art and Life*   9. Margaret and Troy Kinney

                                               10. Cecil Sharp and A. P. Oppé

_ _ _ _ _ *World History of the Dance*   11. Mr. and Mrs. Henry Ford

                                               12. Marjorie Crane Geary

_ _ _ _ _ *The Dance; An Historical Survey of Dancing in Europe*   13. H. Playford

                                               14. Mary Effie Shambaugh

_ _ _ _ _ *Dancing; Ancient and Modern*   15. Elizabeth Rearick

                                               16. Lloyd Shaw

_ _ _ _ _ *A History of Dancing*   17. Beth Tolman and Ralph Page

                                               18. Robert Chambers

_ _ _ _ _ *Peasant Costume in Europe*   19. P. Rameau

                                               20. Jeannette Lincoln

_ _ _ _ _ *Good Morning*

_ _ _ _ _ *Dances of the Hungarians*

_ _ _ _ _ *Folk Dances for Boys and Girls*

_ _ _ _ _ *The Country Dance Book*

_ _ _ _ _ *Cowboy Dances*

_ _ _ _ _ *The Festival Book*

_ _ _ _ _ *Folk Dances of Czechoslovakia*

5. *Rhythmic patterns of basic folk dance steps:*

1. Schottische
2. Polka
3. Waltz
4. Skip
5. Walk
6. Varsovienne
7. Run
8. Step-hop

PART IV. In the blank spaces following each of the descriptive phrases listed below, write the name of the dance to which the phrase to the left best applies and the country which the specific folk dance represents. Consult the list of dances given at the conclusion of this part of the examination for proper spelling of the titles of dances inserted in the right-hand column. You will receive one point for each blank filled in correctly.

	Folk Dance	Country
Example: The dancers wear bells on their costume.	Blue-Eyed Stranger	England
1. A dance performed by friends of the bride before her marriage.	_____	_____
2. The dance harks back to a pagan May Day rite............	_____	_____
3. The man dances with two women; links elbows and skips with first one and then the other.........................	_____	_____
4. A Scandinavian dance similar to the American *Virginia Reel*.	_____	_____
5. The song accompanying this dance tells of an insect which is unable to walk....................................	_____	_____
6. The dance is performed by unmarried girls at country fairs	_____	_____
7. The song accompanying the dance tells of boys who keep money in their shoes.................................	_____	_____
8. Women try to capture a red stocking-cap..................	_____	_____
9. The dance is performed in lines, its title means chain, and it is the national dance of the country represented............	_____	_____
10. The man's partner scolds him unless he is successful in finding a place in a set for them to dance........................	_____	_____
11. The dance combines a polka and a waltz step..............	_____	_____
12. The dance includes a march, a waltz, and a hopsa step......	_____	_____

13. The title refers to "affairs at the inn"..................... _____ _____
14. A dance about a toast........................ _____ _____
15. A dance commemorating the victory of a naval captain in a battle which took place in the St. Lawrence river.......... _____ _____
16. A dance used for hazing university boys.................. _____ _____
17. The man helps his partner spin by flipping her skirts....... _____ _____
18. The title means "chimney sweep"....................... _____ _____
19. One of the movements is a cymbal clash.................. _____ _____
20. The man and woman turn together while dancing although each is performing a different step pattern.................. _____ _____
21. The title of the dance commemorates a hiking trip......... _____ _____
22. A witch doctor calls the change of figures................ _____ _____
23. The title of the dance addresses seamen.................. _____ _____

Black Nag, The	Gustaf's Skoal	Matlanchines, Los
Blue-Eyed Stranger	Hambo	Oxen Dance
Boudigueste, La	Handkerchief Dance	Ril
Come, Let Us Be Joyful	Hull's Victory	Row Well, Ye Mariners
Circle, The	Igüiris, Las	Rufty Tufty
Crested Hen, The	Jabado	Rugen
Csárdás	Kolo	Schuhplattler
Csébogar	Koróboushka	Seven Steps
Cucaracha, La	Kynkkaliepakko	Stoupic, Le
Danish Masquerade	Lauterbach	Virgencita, La
Feiar	Little Man in a Fix	Weggis Dance

PART V. Several selections of folk dance music will be played. After listening to each one, write the meter of the selection (i.e., duple or triple meter), the name of the form (i.e., one-part, two-part, rondo, *et cetera*), and the letters indicating the form (i.e., ABA *et cetera*), in the proper columns provided below. Each selection will be played only two times. You will receive one point for each blank filled in correctly.

	Kind of Meter	*Name of Form*	*Letters Indicating Form*
1.	_____	_____	_____
2.	_____	_____	_____
3.	_____	_____	_____
4.	_____	_____	_____
5.	_____	_____	_____
6.	_____	_____	_____
7.	_____	_____	_____
8.	_____	_____	_____

THE EVALUATION OF SKILL OBJECTIVES

Skills in folk dance may be evaluated by means of any one of several possible methods. The instructor may estimate subjectively the quality of each student's performance or he may use a rating scale for a more refined evaluation of each student's ability. The outline given below lists definite factors included in skill objectives and establishes a standard for what might be judged "excellent" in evaluating performance with respect to each factor.

1. Performance of steps in terms of floor pattern, step pattern, rhythm, accent, and phrasing.
   Describes a clean-cut, accurate floor pattern while dancing. Forward, backward, side-ward, and turning movements are definite and properly spaced. Sharp corner turns or rounded curved paths to be followed are clearly defined.
   Step patterns are accurate with all hops, stamps, jumps, leaps, walking and running steps definite and correctly timed.
   Accents in step patterns are well-defined.
   Folk dance steps, when performed in combinations, are danced as phrases of movement rather than from step to step, e.g., eight waltz steps are danced as a phrase of waltzing rather than as eight separate and disconnected steps.

2. Transitions from phrase to phrase and from figure to figure.
   Transitions from phrase to phrase and from figure to figure are made smoothly and easily so that there is no break in the movement of the folk dance from start to finish. Dancer anticipates each new phrase of movement and performs easily and unhesitatingly throughout the dance. Each phrase is finished completely — that is, no counts of a given step are unfinished and left suspended, thus mitigating against the smooth transition from step to step.

3. Coordination in performance of steps.
   Performance is well-coordinated so that the body is poised and moves rhythmically as one unit; movement of all parts of the body appears to come from one impulse.

4. Range of movement in terms of (a) flexibility and strength in use of feet and legs for eleva-tion, bend of knee, and length of step, (b) bend in torso, and (c) free use of arms in any direction.
   Range of body movement in terms of flexibility and quality is adequate and controlled so that the dancer is capable of good elevation or a slight lift, of a long deep step or of short, delicate steps, of strong, straight arms or of curved, soft arms as indicated by the style of the given folk dance.

5. Style of performance in terms of (a) reproduction of the appropriate quality and spirit of a specific folk dance and (b) body alignment.
   Spirit of each specific dance is accurately and effectively re-created with every perform-ance whether the spirit is vigorous, free, languorous, reserved, fiery, *et cetera*. Use of arms, legs and feet, head, and torso in relation to each other is appropriate in every detail.

61

An instructor wishing to grade students on a purely subjective basis may keep in mind the foregoing concept of a high quality of performance and estimate the status of each student as his performance compares with the standard thus established. An instructor wishing to use a rating scale may assign a value of five points to each of the five factors given in the chart and rate each student in terms of his performance in each of the five skill objectives listed. For example, a student might receive a score of *5* in "(1) Performance of steps," a score of *4* in "(2) Transition from step to step," a score of *4* in "(3) Coordination in performance of steps," a score of *3* in "(4) Range of movement," and a score of *3* in "(5) Style of performance." Thus his total skill score would be *19*. In determining a letter grade for the student, the instructor may follow one of two alternatives:

1. He may arbitrarily establish a numerical range with corresponding letter marks. Since 5 is the highest score which may be awarded for each factor and there are five factors, a perfect score would be 25. On this basis, the following range of scores might be established:

$$23 - 25 - A$$
$$18 - 22 - B$$
$$13 - 17 - C$$
$$8 - 12 - D$$
$$5 - 7 - F$$

This method of grading skill in folk dance compares each student with the ideal standard of performance established and will result, probably, in low marks unless the specific class is highly skilled.

2. He may place the scores of the students in the class in a frequency distribution and base the scores for awarding marks on any one of several accepted methods of grading in terms of a normal curve of distribution which may be found in various books on statistical method.[1] This method of awarding marks is a more relative one than the first method suggested since it compares the performance of students in a specific class with that of other students in their particular group.

A valuable adjunct to the instructor's evaluation of skill in folk dance performance is a form of group grading through which a mark is given each student by other members of the

[1] John F. Bovard and Frederick W. Cozens, *Tests and Measurements in Physical Education* (Philadelphia: W. B. Saunders Company, 1938), Chapters XIII and XVI.

H. Harrison Clarke, *The Application of Measurement to Health and Physical Education* (New York: Prentice-Hall, Inc., 1945), Appendix A.

Henry E. Garrett. *Statistics in Psychology and Education* (New York: Longmans, Green and Co., 1926), Chapters I and VI.

Ruth B. Glassow and Marion R. Broer, *Measuring Achievement in Physical Education* (Philadelphia: W. B. Saunders Company, 1938), Chapter XIII.

Charles Harold McCloy, *Tests and Measurements in Health and Physical Education* (New York: F. S. Crofts and Company, 1939), Chapter XXVI.

M. Gladys Scott and Esther French, *Better Teaching Through Testing* (New York: A. S. Barnes and Company, 1945), Chapter 9.

class who watch his performance and grade him according to previously established concepts of the various possible levels of performance. In establishing the marks to be awarded thus, the instructor should make it clear that a grade of *excellent*, or the traditional *A* rating, signifies the accurate execution of the step pattern involved, good rhythmic phrasing, suitable style of movement for the specific dance, and a sympathetic spirit of participation in the dance itself in keeping with the objectives for skill in folk dance as defined in the preceding outline. Relative marks of *B, C, D,* and *F,* denoting respectively estimates of *good, fair, inferior,* and *failure,* are awarded according to the degree to which each dancer approximates the established standard for an *excellent* performance. Having students grade each other as well as themselves not only affords the teacher a further check on his own somewhat subjective evaluation of his students' performance but results in a salutary effect upon the students themselves in that their observation of others tends to clarify in their own minds the concept of good folk dancing and to motivate a desire to improve in their personal performance. It has the further advantage of emphasizing the social objectives of folk dance with respect to the responsibility of each dancer for the integrity of the performance of a specific folk dance as a whole.

The organization of a folk dance class for purposes of group grading is simple and efficient. Ordinarily, the class should be divided into groups of six. If the formation for the dance to be tested requires eight people, the number of groups should be adjusted so that there will be eight groups; however, there should be at least six individuals assigned to each group to insure greater reliability in this particular method of grading. Each student is given a grading form (See Diagram 1, page 64) with his group number and letter to be used for identification purposes within his group inserted on the form thus prepared. On this form, he grades the other members in his group. For example, the student whose grading form is shown in the diagram is person *a* in *Group I.* Diagram 2, page 65, shows a convenient arrangement of the class upon the floor. All *a's* perform and are graded in turn by the members of their respective groups. They are followed by the *b's, c's, d's, e's,* and *f's* in turn. Students award marks on a numerical basis—5 for *excellent* or *A,* 4 for *good* or *B,* 3 for *fair* or *C,* 2 for *poor* or *D,* and 1 for *very poor (failure)* or *F.* Diagram 3, page 67, illustrates the grading forms as used by Group I of a folk dance class which is tested on the performance of the *Danish Schottische,* the *Finnish Polka, The Crested Hen, Kynklaliepakko,* and the *Hambo.* Three methods are possible for determining the final score to be awarded to each student for his performance in each dance or skill tested.

1. The grade most often awarded may be designated as his mark and the numerical value translated into a letter grade. For example, *a's* scores on the *Hambo,* as awarded by *b, c, d, e,* and *f* in his particular group, are *4, 4, 4, 5,* and *5,* respectively. Therefore, *a's* score on the *Hambo* is recorded as *B*—the letter grade for a mark of *4*—since his performance was given a grade of *4* three times and a grade of *5* only twice. This method is a simple one but becomes confusing at times when the agreement among five graders is not consistent. For example, the scores of a specific individual might read *3, 3, 4, 2, 4,* in which case 3 is the final score which probably should be awarded but actually there is no majority score.

Group _I_

Dancer _a_

Name _George Bailey_

Date _October 27, 1947_

Score _____ Grade _____

	a
	b
	c
	d
	e
	f

Scale for Grading:

Excellent -- 5
Good -------- 4
Fair ------- 3
Poor ------- 2
Very Poor -- 1

Factors to be considered in evaluating over-all performance:

1. Performance of steps in dances in terms of floor pattern, step pattern, rhythm, accent, and phrasing.
2. Transitions from step to step and from figure to figure.
3. Coordination in performance of steps.
4. Range of body movement in terms of flexibility and quality.
5. Style of performance in terms of reproduction of appropriate quality and spirit and of accurate body alignment.

Diagram 1—Form for group grading.

2. A second method for determining letter marks based upon the numerical scores awarded by a group is the comparison of each individual score with an arbitrary standard recommended as the first of two possible methods for grading by an instructor of a class in folk dance. For the skill test illustrated in the diagram, there are five scores awarded each student (one for each of the five dances) and five different individuals are grading each performance. Thus the highest score which any student may achieve is *125*, or 5 (highest single mark) × 5 (the number of dances being tested) × 5 (the number of students grading each dancer).

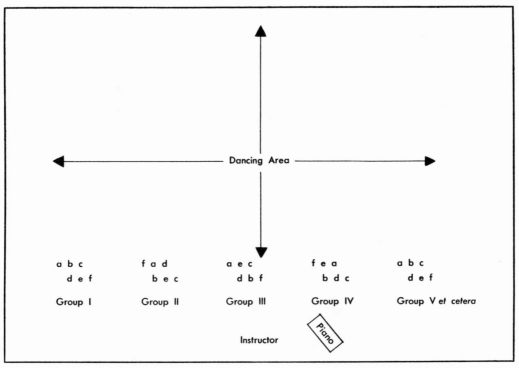

Diagram 2 — Arrangement of class on the floor for purposes of group grading.

On this basis, the following range of scores may be established:

$$113 - 125 - A$$
$$88 - 112 - B$$
$$63 - 87 - C$$
$$38 - 62 - D$$
$$25 - 37 - F$$

3. A third method for the awarding of marks in an evaluation of folk dance skills may be based upon a normal curve of distribution. By this method, *a's* numerical score on the *Hambo* — a score of 22 — may be placed in a frequency distribution of scores made by all of the students tested on the *Hambo* if that were the only dance being tested. If a single skill grade is sought for a test which covers several dances, as at the close of a specific unit of folk dances or at the close of a six-weeks period of study, the instructor may arrive at a single grade by totaling the scores given by each student for

all of the dances graded as illustrated at the bottom of Diagram 3, page 67. For example, on this particular practical test including five Scandinavian dances, *a's* total scores on all five dances are 24, 23, 24, 25, and 24 as awarded by *b, c, d, e,* and *f,* respectively, giving him a grand total score of 120 on the entire test. The total scores for the entire test made by other members of Group I are *b*—95, *c*—60, *d*—93, *e*—64, and *f*—121. These scores may be arranged in a frequency distribution with scores made by all students in the class and letter grades awarded on the basis of any one of several statistically approved methods for determining letter marks from numerical scores which have been placed in a frequency distribution. Diagram 4 illustrates a purely hypothetical distribution of such scores with letter marks established on the basis of the median and the upper and lower quartiles, at the same time keeping in mind the normal breaks in the scores of the frequency distribution into which they have been grouped.

According to the letter grades determined on the basis of a normal curve of distribution, *a's* grade on the test is A, *b* receives a grade of B, and *c, d, e,* and *f* receive grades of D—, B, C—, and A, respectively. In using this method of group grading, the instructor should grade each pupil and use grades given by students for checking the validity of his own evaluations. It is the experience of the authors that grades awarded by students correlate very closely with those given by the instructor *if* the students participating in such a project are familiar with the dances and have a clear concept of exactly what constitutes the excellent performance of each specific dance with varying degrees of performance related thereto.

Another method of grading performance in folk dance which may be used occasionally is that of tabulating errors. Each time a student errs in his performance of a dance, the individual watching him scores a mark beside his name on the form provided. Students should be clear in their understanding of what constitutes the errors to be tallied thus—that is, incorrect execution of step or figure, inaccurate timing of specific step patterns, failure to make transitions smoothly, *et cetera*. When all students have been tested thus, grades may be awarded by giving the individual with the fewest errors an *A* with grades of *B, C, D,* and *F* awarded either in a relative manner or awarded on the basis of a standard of errors for each mark of A, B, C, D, or F according to a previously established scale. This method of evaluation, however, is somewhat negative in its approach and should be used only occasionally when accuracy is the primary factor for consideration.

At no time should the achievement of marks or grades be permitted to rank as the primary objective in a folk dance class; however, since joy in participation is heightened with good performance, it is highly desirable that students are motivated at all times to become better dancers. Other things being equal, it is a generally accepted truism that students tend to enjoy and to repeat those activities in which they are more or less highly skilled.

EVALUATION OF THE TEACHING OF FOLK DANCE

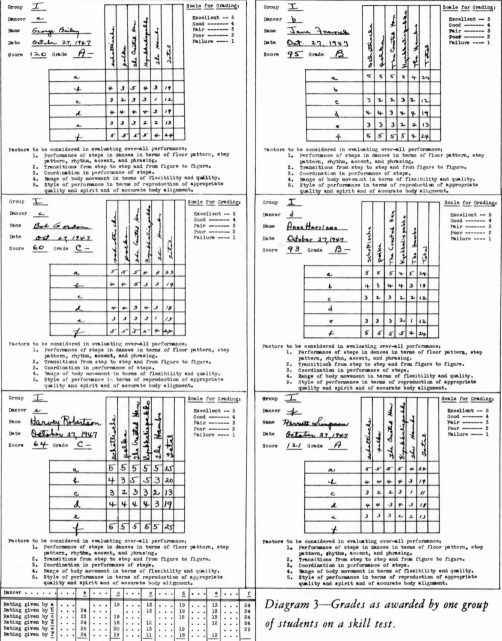

Dancer	a	b	c	d	e	f
Rating given by a		19	12	19	13	24
Rating given by b	24		12	19	13	24
Rating given by c	23	19		18	13	24
Rating given by d	24	18	12		12	24
Rating given by e	25	20	13	19		25
Rating given by f	24	19	11	18	13	
Total Score	120	95	60	93	64	121

Diagram 3—Grades as awarded by one group of students on a skill test.

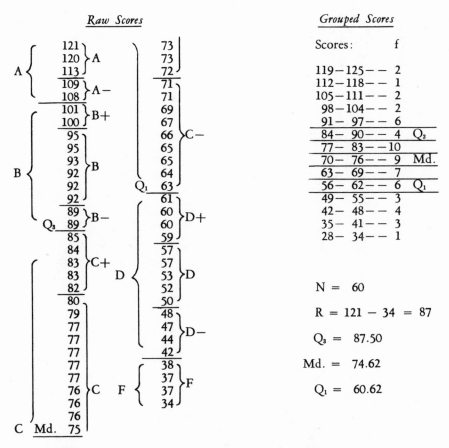

Diagram 4 — Illustrative example of a frequency distribution of hypothetical scores on a test for the purpose of evaluating skills in folk dance with the assignment of letter grades based upon approved statistical procedures.

EVALUATION OF ATTITUDE AND APPRECIATION OBJECTIVES

Attitudes and appreciations are somewhat intangible but constitute very important outcomes of the leadership in folk dance activities. The most valid method of evaluating attitudes and appreciations is that of observing the spirit of participation on the part of those involved, the amount of interest demonstrated, and the rapidity with which actual learning takes place. Standardized tests in this area of evaluation are not available at the present time. In their absence, however, it is the opinion of the authors of *The Folk Dance Library* that attitudes and appreciations are directly related to knowledges acquired and to the skills developed. In other words, those who acquire the greatest amount of information and who evince the most superior skills with respect to this phase of the school and college curriculum usually have, by the same token, developed the best attitudes and appreciations established as specific objectives for the study of folk dance.

So that the instructor may have in mind the important attitudes and appreciations to be fostered through folk dance and may impart these concepts to his students, the following outline, presenting factors included in attitude and appreciation objectives with criteria for evaluating them, is suggested.

1. Joy in group and individual participation.
   Enjoys dancing solo folk dances and enjoys the fellowship and oneness of spirit which comes from participation in group folk dances.
2. Utilization of time before the beginning of a class and practice periods interspersed during class periods for the perfection of individual skills or for helping others in perfecting these skills.
   Utilizes time before class begins and periods given during class to the maximum in the perfection of his own performance in terms of accuracy and quality or spirit, and in helping fellow dancers with different skills so that they are able to improve their individual performance.
3. Individual responsibility as a reliable dancer in a group.
   Assumes responsibility for his specific place in every group dance in terms of spacing his movements in all directions so that the design formed by the group as a whole is preserved, reaching to complete the formation of circles as soon as possible for the sake of design and safety, maintaining a secure grasp on other dancers when executing movements involving high speed or momentum, being especially conscientious about the accurate performance of a folk dance step when dancing with a partner to preclude his confusion and resultant dissatisfaction.
4. Cooperation as a member of a group.
   Participates whole-heartedly in every performance of a folk dance so that he contributes to a group feeling in the re-creation of the spirit of the dance.
   Moves alertly and intelligently during the learning of new dances, concentrates on directions so as to help the group as a whole to enjoy the entire dance as quickly as possible.
5. Value of folk dance in the culture of a people.
   Appreciates the contributions made by folk dance to the culture of folk groups in their celebration of festivals which are both sacred and secular in nature.
6. Dance as an adult skill.
   Appreciates dance as a skill respected by folk peoples everywhere for men, women, and children as participants and as a skill in which mastery is sought, especially by adults.
7. Physiological values of folk dance.
   Appreciates the physiological values of folk dance in terms of an optimum state of

69

organic vigor, the development of good musculature, coordination, balance, and a beautiful quality of body movement in general.

8. Mental values of folk dance.

Appreciates the mental values to be gained through folk dance in terms of a healthy, normal outlet for strains and tensions, opportunity for expression of creative impulses through participation in dances involving a wide range of emotional qualities, and a feeling of security which results from the unity of spirit present in group participation in folk dance.

9. The people of the world and especially of the United States.

Appreciates keenly the various racial groups of people in the world through palpable participation in their folk dances. Realizes a deeper understanding of these groups and especially the various separate groups who migrated to the United States to settle this country, bringing a rich cultural heritage of folk dance to their adopted country.

Chapter 6
The Production of Folk Festivals and Folk Dance Parties

PROCEDURES IN THE PRODUCTION OF FOLK FESTIVALS AND FOLK DANCE PARTIES

The folk festival is an ancient, universal celebration for the corporate expression by all peoples of joy, thanksgiving, praise, and similar emotions associated with the commemoration of both sacred and secular occasions. The sources for these group celebrations throughout history are legion: the advent of spring, bringing release from the hardships of winter; the harvesting of crops; the recurrence of religious holidays; the gathering together for sharing participation in some form of expression such as music, dance, drama, or athletic activities; the commemoration of an event of great historical importance. The celebration of traditional folk festivals has taken as many forms as there have been groups to celebrate them; the mode of celebration, however, has reflected always the life of the people of a given time and place, resulting in the fact that the characteristics of a specific festival celebrated in any country for a period of centuries show variations in its form from time to time.

All folk festivals, however, have certain factors in common: (1) the festival stems from one cause, idea, or event which is its *raison d'être*, (2) the activities which are included in the festival are traditional in nature although they may be altered or may change gradually over a period of many years, and (3) the organization of the festival is such that all who attend do so in the capacity of participants; some take part more actively than others, to be sure, but without the gathering together of the people involved and the general participation on the part of all, there would be no festival.

A genuine folk festival is one which is indigenous to the culture of the locality in which it is held. A real English May Day festival can be celebrated only by Englishmen on the appointed day in England or in another country where Englishmen have settled and thus perpetuate the customs of their homeland through celebrations brought to the adopted country along with other traditional patterns of living. It would be impossible for people in the state of Washington, for example, to celebrate an orange festival and just as unlikely that Florida might hold an apple festival. Texans celebrate March 2 as the anniversary of the Independence of Texas, but there would be no cause for West Virginians to celebrate this particular date as such. Festivals, no matter how large or how small, are real or genuine festivals to the extent to which they grow out of the lives of the people who celebrate them. Thus a genuine festival may be seasonal, historical, religious, economic, or patriotic in its origin.

Participation in folk festivals is a thoroughly logical and highly significant experience for those enrolled in folk dance classes under the auspices of an educational or recreational organization. Because the potentialities of their contributions to the realization of the objectives of folk dance established in Chapter 2 of the present volume are limitless, full scope for the development of folk festivals should be explored by those in charge of this phase of the school or recreation program. Such festivals may take the form of those indigenous to the particular community, making copious use of the folk dances with which these celebrations are commemorated traditionally, or they may take the form of a re-enactment of folk festivals stemming from other times and places. Thus a particular school, college, or community may commemorate in a festal celebration its history or a particular episode, product, or occasion for which the specific community is well known and therefore unique. This type of festival is planned so that all who attend do so in the capacity of participants. The outline for a proposed Corn-Husking Bee, which follows later in the present chapter, illustrates this type of celebration.

Folk festivals, as an important phase of an educational or recreational program, should not be confined necessarily to those of an indigenous nature. Frequently, the theme and traditions of a foreign festival may be borrowed and re-enacted so that those participating may re-live experiences which have been considered worthwhile by other groups of people and, through such experiences, students of folk dance may become more intimately acquainted with the customs of the people of another time and place. Thus, a celebration sponsored by any American school or community may take the form of a re-enactment of a traditional festal celebration by peoples of other times and places, utilizing activities in the form of dances, games, songs, dramas, contests, costumes, special characters, decorations, and all subsidiary adjuncts to the festival originally celebrated elsewhere. This type of festival should grow out of classes in folk dance and should be planned and rehearsed by those participating. Others who attend do so in the capacity of spectators with the privilege of seeing a re-enactment of a traditional and authentic festival from another time and place. A celebration of this kind necessitates the preparation of a script so that it moves along smoothly as a spontaneous affair. Those participating, however, are aware of cues in the script which tell them when to begin each new activity. The English May Day Festival outlined in the present chapter illustrates this particular type of celebration. Such festivals may be termed — for want of a better name — *pseudo-festivals* as opposed to those of an indigenous nature. Although the so-called pseudo-festival can never be considered a genuine, real festival, it should incorporate the traditions of the indigenous festival so that the spirit of the original event is experienced in essence which is, after all, the most important aspect of any celebration. Thus it may prove broadening in its educational experiences through which understanding is quickened and appreciation of heritage is fostered.

Another use of folk materials which enables students to experience folk dances, songs, and games in their proper settings is a typical folk dance party. In planning such a party, the activities may or may not be confined to a specific historical event in the history of the given country, to a particular season, or to a special holiday. In other words, folk dance parties may be planned in conjunction with a special season or occasion in a specific country, or they may be planned as a social gathering only, illustrative of a party representative of the people of a particular country at any time. For this reason, greater liberty may be exercised in the bringing together of activities which do not share a unity of time and place as far as a traditional cele-bration is concerned. Such parties should, however, have a unity of idea. For example, a party may be planned to demonstrate customs and activities associated with the celebration of Christmas in various countries. In this type of party, a unity of time or place is impossible; the theme of Christmas, however, ties the celebration together. All activities included in any kind of folk dance party should be authentic in origin. The *Noche Mexicana*, a Mexican folk dance party which is outlined in the present chapter, illustrates this type of folk dance party.

In the four volumes of *The Folk Dance Library* devoted to the presentation of folk dance materials, occasions for festal celebrations of various countries are reviewed briefly. These occasions, in turn, may serve as the nuclei of folk festivals and parties for those interested in developing them as culminating activities in conjunction with the completion of the various units of folk dances presented. The basic principles for the production of folk festivals and folk dance parties, and the illustrative scripts which follow in this chapter, may serve as further guides for the successful planning of these particular projects.

While certain basic principles for the production of a folk festival or folk dance party are established in the ensuing pages, one overlying principle should obtain — the maintenance of unity with respect to idea or theme so that the resultant activities do not present a hodge-podge of folk dances for the primary purpose of exhibition on the part of those participating actively. In other words, the indigenous festival or the festival resulting from the re-enact-ment of a traditional celebration representative of those of other times and places can prove enriching and creative as an experience only to the extent to which a semblance of unity of idea or theme, careful allegiance to the authenticity of detail, and wise provision for the par-ticipation of all concerned prevail. The production of a folk festival or of a folk dance party has larger ends to serve than those which so often obtain when the primary purpose of the presentation — worthy as it may be as one phase of promoting better understanding of a folk dance program and subsequent improved public relations for its support — is for demonstration only of an isolated series of dances learned.

The celebration of any folk festival or folk dance party should provide some form of par-ticipation for all who attend. There should be activities planned for the occasion which are so simple that everyone may join in them. Songs, contests, games, and simple folk dances are illustrative of types of activity which are highly suitable for general participation. Group singing, under a good leader, of songs which are authentic with respect to the particular time and place serving as the setting for the folk festival or party may be supplemented by songs presented through collaboration with the Department of Music in an educational institution or by a special interest group in this area of a civic or recreational organization. The same principle applies to the use of folk dance as an activity with which the particular festival or party is celebrated. In the course of the festival, special groups may present more advanced, ritualistic or ceremonial dances, appropriate to the occasion celebrated, to supplement the general participation in simpler dances on the part of all involved. Appropriate plays or dramas may be woven into the festival script in collaboration with the Department of Speech or Drama in an educational institution or a similar special interest group in recreational or civic organizations.

In all activities planned for general participation, leadership is highly important in insuring their success. For group singing, song sheets, with the words of the songs to be used, should be prepared in advance and distributed to all for this phase of the festival or party program. They may be mimeographed or printed and should serve to carry out the spirit of the occasion itself if special attention is given to color and decorative motifs.

The decorations used for the setting of the festival or folk dance party may contribute richly to the spirit of the occasion and to the establishment of a tone or quality for the specific celebration. They should be carefully chosen as to authenticity and ingeniously executed. While they need not represent a literal duplication of the authentic setting for a particular festival, the decorations can and should present the essence of the original setting re-enacted.

A valuable aspect of any festival occasion is an arrangement of exhibits which may display folk arts and crafts, authentic relics of interest which are pertinent to the occasion, reproductions of authentic articles, and special products relative to the specific celebration.

The refreshments which are served, whether they are free or must be purchased, are more interesting if they are authentic. For the re-enactment of pseudo-festivals of a former day, it may not be feasible to duplicate foods exactly; however, these traditional festal foods should be approximated as closely as possible.

In summary, the following guiding principles for the production of folk festivals and folk dance parties are suggested:

1. The festival should have one central idea or theme upon which it is built.

2. There should be some activities for all who are participating in the festival.

3. All activities included in the festival should have some authentic relationship to the traditional festival on which the re-enactment is based.

4. Entertainment should be provided which presents authentic material demonstrating folk songs, dances and dramas which demand skilled performers.

5. Refreshments should be served or sold which are in keeping with the traditional foods associated with the particular celebration.

6. The production of the festival should be carried out by committees with specific duties which function under a general Steering Committee in charge of the over-all plans for the celebration.

The last principle listed is essential to the planning and implementation of a successful festival based upon folk materials. The most expedient method of organization for these functions is the establishment of a Steering Committee with the responsibility for allocating duties to various, specific committees and to seeing that the festival is planned and executed through the collaboration of all individuals and groups represented on these committees. In the final analysis, the chairman of the Steering Committee is the person, more than anyone else, who is responsible for the successful production of the folk festival or folk dance party undertaken.

Following the folk festival or folk dance party, each committee should compile a report of its activities and expenditures along with suggestions for improvement of the celebration to be filed with the Steering Committee for future reference. A specific form for making these reports established in advance by the Steering Committee is highly advisable. If the same festival or party is to be celebrated again, reports from the initial experience will make the work of the various committees both simpler and more efficacious.

STEERING COMMITTEE

The duties of the Steering Committee, arranged in a logical order for their execution, are as follows:

1. Select the date for the festival or party—unless the date is arbitrary, such as Hallowe'en or May Day; even then, it might be wise for the success of the festival to substitute another date. The calendar of activities for the school or community should be checked carefully for other events which might offer competition to participation in the festival. Conflict with large gatherings sponsored by church or civic groups, especially if the town is small, should be avoided, as well as other important events scheduled on the school or college calendar. Announce the date of the festival as soon after it has been selected as possible.

2. Select the site of the festival. Specifications for the site depend upon the particular nature of the celebration itself. Some are more suited to outdoor observance, others to indoor celebration. Often a combination of indoor and outdoor areas is desirable. If the Steering Committee selects an out-of-doors site for the festival, an alternate inside area should be selected in event inclement weather makes the outdoor celebration inadvisable. Alternate plans for an indoor festival seem more desirable than the confusion which results from last minute postponement. Psychologically, the deferment of a festival gives the ultimate celebration of it something of the quality of an anti-climax.

3. Outline the events of the folk festival or party in a general way in terms of types of activities and sequence of events. Allot time in terms of actual minutes or hours which are to be allowed for each part of the festival or party program. The details of planning these various parts of the program should be left to committees appointed for that specific purpose in collaboration with the Steering Committee for the project as a whole.

4. Determine the number and types of committees necessary for the successful production of the folk festival or folk dance party. The choice of committees depends upon the type of festival or party to be produced. In general, however, the following committees and sub-committees are necessary:

a. *Steering Committee*
    (1) Finance Committee

b. *Research Committee*

c. *Hospitality Committee*
    (1) Invitations Committee

d. *Publicity Committee*
    (1) Newspaper Publicity Committee
    (2) Poster Committee
    (3) Photography Committee
    (4) Stunt Publicity Committee

e. *Program Committee*
    (1) Dance Committee
    (2) Games and Contests Committee
    (3) Music Committee
    (4) Costume Committee
    (5) Dramatics Committee

f. *Grounds Committee*
    (1) Exhibits Committee
    (2) Decorations Committee
    (3) Construction Committee
    (4) Properties Committee

g. *Foods Committee*

5. Appoint committee chairmen and members of the various committees serving under the chairmanship of each committee appointed. Some committees will need more members than others. It is desirable that as many people as possible be included in the preparations for the proposed folk festival or folk dance party; the membership of planning committees is an important aspect of the project in which many individuals may serve to the mutual advantage of the project as a whole and to that of those responsible for its success. It then becomes the responsibility of each committee chairman to direct the contributions of the personnel of his particular committee to the successful realization of goals established for the occasion.

6. Integrate the efforts of all committees. This is one of the most important functions of the Steering Committee because both the facility and pleasure with which the folk festival or party is produced and its ultimate success depend upon the integration of the efforts of all concerned in its production. The first step in the coordination of committee work is an initial meeting of the Steering Committee with the chairmen of all other committees to discuss over-all plans and procedures for the particular project.

7. Receive requests from committees for all materials and equipment to be purchased for use in the festival or party and to arrange for the payment for such supplies. This is the direct responsibility of the Sub-Committee on Finance of the Steering Committee. The means for financing a folk festival or party vary in different situations. Frequently, a small admission fee is charged those attending the celebration. Sometimes the profit from foods sold is utilized to defray the expenses entailed. Occasionally, if the festival is planned definitely as a learning situation for students in a high school or college, the funds necessary for its production are ear-marked as such in the school or college budget.

8. Prepare for the chairman of each committee a map to indicate the location of events and a program showing the sequence of these events. These maps may be distributed after the Program Committee has developed the details for the entire program for the folk festival or folk dance party.

9. Give the Publicity Committee pertinent data regarding the festival in ample time for its members to initiate an effective publicity campaign.

10. Prepare and distribute forms for the chairmen of each committee to use in making a report of the activities performed by their respective committees with suggestions for improving or facilitating the work of the group as a whole.

11. Send "thank you" letters to individuals, other than those serving directly on various committees, who assisted in the production of the festival or party. This list of personnel will, of course, vary according to the particular situation; however, it usually includes:

   a. Administrative officers of the school or college and civic officials in the community.

   b. School or campus workmen who assisted in the construction, decoration, moving of properties, *et cetera*.

   c. Judges of contests included in the festival or folk dance party.

   d. Proprietors of stores in which posters were placed to advertise the festival.

   e. Any other individuals who contributed to the festival in good measure, including especially those whose background enabled them to contribute authentic information, properties, or atmosphere to the celebration of the folk festival or party.

RESEARCH COMMITTEE

The Research Committee is responsible for collecting all data possible pertaining to the history of the particular folk festival or party and the celebration of similar festivals held in other schools, colleges, or communities. The specific duties of this group are as follows:

1. Gather data regarding the history and background of the proposed festival or party from books, magazines, files of newspapers, and any other available printed sources.

2. Interview individuals living in the community who, because of personal experience or unusual background, are qualified to give authentic information regarding the particular festival or folk dance party to be presented.

3. Make available for consultation by all committees a report of the results of the research undertaken and completed.

4. Be ready to find the answer, if possible, to any questions which committees may raise to which answers may not be found in the prepared material presented for their convenience in carrying out their respective duties.

HOSPITALITY COMMITTEE

The members of the Hospitality Committee serve as hosts and hostesses for the folk festival or folk dance party. Specifically, they should:

1. Make arrangements for housing guests if the celebration includes participants or guests from out-of-town areas.

2. Issue invitations for participation in the festival to special groups in the community such as ministers, city officials, and administrators in the public schools and college.

3. Greet guests as they arrive at the site of the festival.

4. See that all in attendance at the festival or party are encouraged to participate and are aided in finding a place to engage in dancing, contests, singing, *et cetera*.

The Hospitality Committee may appoint a Sub-Committee on Invitations to be responsible for designing and executing the invitations themselves. Invitations are more colorful and festive for this purpose if they depart from formal written or printed ones in favor of decorative motifs, shapes, or patterns in keeping with the theme underlying the folk festival or party. Invitations should include information regarding (1) the occasion, (2) the place, (3) the date, (4) the time, (5) the admission fee (if any), (6) types of costumes which are suitable to be worn.

PUBLICITY COMMITTEE

The chief duty of the Publicity Committee is that of acquainting the public with the details of the folk festival or folk dance party. This information may be divided into such areas as (1) the history and background of the folk festival or party; (2) the place, date, hour, and admission fee (if any) for this project; (3) content of the program, including events open to all who attend as well as attractions to be featured for special purposes of entertainment; (4) personnel responsible for the production of the festival, that is, committee personnel. The Publicity Committee is responsible, also, for soliciting data from each of the various committees prior to the festival and far enough in advance to enable the publicity to reach everyone who should be acquainted with the event. The work of the Publicity Committee may be expedited by dividing the group into the following sub-committees with specific duties to perform:

1. *Newspaper Publicity Committee*

   a. Place a feature article announcing the folk festival or party in appropriate newspapers, i.e. — the school or college paper if the festival is limited to a scholastic situation, in the school paper and the local city papers if the affair is open to the public, and in the papers of surrounding cities if participation in the festival is to encompass a larger area than those listed above. This announcement feature should be released at least three weeks prior to the date of the folk festival or party and should present the types of activities to be included in the program.

   b. Provide newspapers with feature articles on the background of the festival or party, human interest stories regarding preparations for the occasion, and articles on personnel responsible for the production of the festival or party during the weeks which follow the initial announcement.

   c. Release detailed information regarding the program, including specific activities, sequence of events and featured attractions, about one week before the festival or party date.

2. *Poster Committee*

   a. Make or arrange, through art classes in a school or college situation or through groups of talented individuals within the community, for the making of posters to be placed in stores or buildings where individuals who are free to participate in or to attend the festival or party may see them. Posters should be designed in keeping with the central theme of the festival or party. Illustrations on posters can be of great value in suggesting types of costumes to be worn for the occasion.

   b. See that posters include all important data such as date, hour, place, and fee, if any, regarding participation or attendance.

3. *Photography Committee*

   a. Take pre-festival publicity pictures of individuals dressed in costume and engaging in typical activities or review files of previous similar festivals for pictures which might be used for publicity purposes.

   b. Provide newspapers with publicity pictures. These probably should be turned over to the newspaper publicity committee so that only one contact is made with the local papers.

   c. Take pictures during the festival of:

1. Costumes	5. Musicians
2. Contests and contest winners	6. Judges
3. Dancing	7. Other groups or activities which
4. Dramatic presentations	have human interest appeal

4. *Stunt Publicity Committee*

   a. Devise various means of publicizing the festival such as (1) skits to be given in school or college assemblies, before the Parent-Teachers' Association, men's luncheon clubs, or similar organizations, (2) a parade which might march through the main streets of the town or about a school campus, *et cetera.*

   b. Arrange exhibits advertising the festival or party which may be placed in strategic spots such as the foyers of public buildings.

PROGRAM COMMITTEE

The Program Committee is responsible for all of the actual events of the folk festival or folk dance party. Because the work of this committee is so heavy and so important, the division of the group into sub-committees to assume responsibility for each of the various aspects of the folk festival or party program is desirable. The Program Committee should meet as a whole from time to time to discuss procedures and to integrate the festival activities. When all activities have been planned by each of the sub-committees, a sequence of events for the entire festival or party should be outlined and passed on to the Steering and Publicity Committees. The sub-committees of the Program Committee and a list of their specific responsibilities are as follows:

1. *Dance Committee*

   a. Select dances in which the individuals attending the festival will participate. Dances chosen to be learned and performed by the group in attendance should be fairly short, simple in step pattern and in design, should involve small units of

79

dancers, i.e., couples, or sets of four, eight, or twelve, and should reach their climaxes quickly, in order to insure satisfaction accruing from participation.

b. Select personnel to direct the dances. If the dances must be taught to the group participating in the festival or party, outline definite methods and procedures for teaching them. This particular part of the program is most important. The individual selected to direct the dances must be someone who is skilled in handling large groups of people. He or she must be able to give clear, brief, simple directions and capable of reducing the procedures for teaching these dances to a minimum of time.

c. Organize a floor plan for the arrangement of participants on the dancing area. This plan for organization is very important to insure the smoothness of the festival or party but should not be too laborious for the dancers to adapt to it. Methods of this type of organization vary; however, one simple, effective method involves marking the dancing area into sections with enough space in each section to accommodate one set composed of the number of individuals needed to dance the folk dance requiring the largest single unit such as a quadrille for eight, a longways set with six or seven couples, *et cetera*. Encourage those who attend the festival and who wish to participate in the dancing to come in sets, giving the leader of each set the number of the dancing area upon which it will perform. Special provision should be made to place those who come alone or without previous allocation to specific sets into those sets which are incomplete. This may be done quickly by having those dancers without definite places in sets to come to a designated spot. The individual in charge of the folk dances then may call for a show of hands wherever sets are incomplete, and those without places may fill in these sets. It is advisable to have couples designated as "roving couples" on hand to dance in any sets which are incomplete after all guests have been given places to dance.

d. Arrange for a group of skilled, previously coached dancers to serve as a demonstration set. This group should appear in appropriate costume and should be prepared to give those learning the dances an accurate picture of how each dance or part of a dance should look when properly performed. Demonstration sets should perform on a platform or in a special area facilitating observation of their performance. In event a platform is not available, the dancers on the floor may stoop or sit down in place so that the demonstration set may be seen by all.

e. Arrange for all special dancing to be presented as entertainment by skilled groups of performers. These dances should represent folk dances traditionally associated with the folk festival or party which are too difficult for participation on the part of the crowds attending. The Dance Committee may be responsible for teaching the special dances to this group or may delegate this responsibility to others.

2. *Games and Contests Committee*
   a. Determine the number and kinds of games or contests to be included in keeping with the amount of time allocated for this type of event.
   b. Plan the space needed for each game or contest in keeping with the areas designated for this purpose and draw up a diagram indicating location, length, width, and color of all lines to be marked, specifications for equipment to be provided, *et cetera*. This diagram should be given to the Grounds Committee in ample time for them to prepare the grounds prior to the folk festival or party.
   c. Select judges for the contests. Notify them of their duties and of the time and place of the contests they are to judge. The position of the judges of contests at a large festival of this type is considered by most people who are invited to serve as an assignment of prestige; the judges, therefore, should be given some mark of distinction such as a large, decorative badge. Unless the judges are very familiar with the types of contests included in the festival, it is necessary to establish definite criteria as guides for their selection of the best song, the best play, the best churning technique, *et cetera*.
   d. Appoint someone to direct the contests, announce the names of those entering, give signals, and make this part of the festival enjoyable for spectators as well as for contestants. If a large number of people are expected to enter the various contests, it is advisable to have preliminary contests on the evening before the festival, or at some time prior to the festival, and to hold only the contest finals on the date of the festival itself.
   e. Establish rules for all contests. The nature of each contest and the rules for entering should be publicized well in advance and a date for entering the contests made known so that entries may be handled efficiently and the contests themselves conducted in an orderly manner.
3. *Music Committee*
   a. Determine type of accompaniment needed for dancing, singing, entertainment, or background effects and make arrangements to provide this by means of musicians or by records.
   b. Arrange for musicians. Acquaint them with time and place where they are to play, any particular type of costume which they are to wear, and the specific selections which they are to play. If necessary, the musicians should be provided with arrangements of the music selected.
   c. Plan a list of songs to be sung by the group in keeping with the amount of time set aside for group singing. The words to these songs should be printed or mimeographed and distributed to the crowd for the period of singing.
   d. Select a skilled director to lead the group singing. Acquaint him or her with the hour, place, and length of time set aside for singing as well as the songs which are to be sung. Often the person who is to lead the singing is a member of the Program Committee and assists in planning the songs.

   e. Arrange for any special music to be used as entertainment. Traditional folk music associated with the festival which is too elaborate for the group as a whole to sing may be sung by a chorus, as a solo, or played as special instrumental selections.

 4. *Costume Committee*

   a. Give to Publicity Committee details regarding appropriate costumes to be worn to the festival or party with suggestions as to how the costumes may be made or assembled simply and easily.

   b. Assume responsibility for providing costumes for those who are appearing in a demonstration dance set, a play or skit, or in any other capacity as entertainment for the folk festival or party. The costumes may be rented, borrowed, or made. If they must be made, it is the duty of the Costume Committee either to supervise the making or actually to make the costumes. If the latter plan is followed, the Committee is responsible for taking measurements, arranging for fittings, and seeing the costumes through to completion before the festival itself.

 5. *Dramatics Committee*

   a. Select dramatic material to be used as a part of the program. Any short plays or scenes from plays should be in keeping with the theme of the festival and should contribute to its authenticity. Not every celebration of this kind will have a place for a play; dramatic presentations, however, are very definitely a part of many types of festivals.

   b. Cast characters for the play and be responsible for producing it.

   c. Design and execute any special lighting effects for any part of the festival.

GROUNDS COMMITTEE

   The Grounds Committee is responsible for the mechanics of preparing the site of the festival for the particular celebration. This is an important and prodigious task and requires a large committee of individuals who are dependable, ingenious, and capable. This committee transforms the site into a festival scene and restores it to its normal state following the celebration. For greater efficiency, the tasks of this committee are delegated to sub-committees as follows:

 1. *Exhibits Committee*

   a. Plan exhibits of interest to those attending the festival. These may be collections of authentic articles which pertain to the festival or they may be replicas of authentic pieces. The exhibits should be arranged attractively and, wherever possible, they should be presented in a setting which makes a unit rather than spread out in rows on tables. For example, the semblance of a room in a pioneer cabin might be the background for exhibiting interesting articles as part of a festival built about Early America.

   b. Arrange for articles to be exhibited; assume responsibility for procuring them and for returning them to the owners from whom they are borrowed.

    c. Set up the exhibits; if necessary, arrange for someone to be on hand during the festival to supervise the exhibits and to answer questions regarding them.

2. *Decorations Committee*

    a. Decorate the site of the festival in keeping with the theme of the celebration with careful adherence to authentic and suitable types of decoration. While the decorations are of great importance in establishing the spirit and mood of the festival, they should in no way interfere with its progress. The purpose of decorations at a folk festival or party is to re-create, as far as possible, the *spirit* or *essence* of the authentic setting for festivals of the type undertaken.

3. *Construction Committee*

    a. Assume responsibility for all construction requested by any other committee. This work, which includes all lines to be drawn, platforms to be built, necessary painting, arrangements of electric lighting to be set up, *et cetera*, may be supervised by the members of the committee or actually executed by them.

    b. Remove all temporary structures following the festival.

4. *Properties Committee*

    a. Procure any properties needed by other committees.

    b. Return all properties to owners following the festival.

Foods Committee

The Foods Committee plans, arranges for, and serves any refreshments to be sold or served free to guests during the course of the folk festival or party. As nearly as possible and feasible, the foods served should be the kind enjoyed traditionally by those celebrating the festival in its original setting or should represent a contemporary adaptation of these foods.

ILLUSTRATIVE FOLK FESTIVALS

An American Corn-Husking Bee

The Corn-Husking Bee, as an indigenous American festival, grew out of the work life of the pioneers of this country. Corn, or maize—the "source of life" given to the settlers of America by the Indians—became one of the chief staples in the diet of our pioneers. Years in which the corn crop was poor proved lean ones, indeed. A short crop of corn throughout the land meant famine and suffering during the bitter months of winter; it was this adversity among others that very nearly caused the failure of the Pilgrim Fathers to establish a settlement on the New England coast of this country. The abundant crop of corn which ended this early danger prompted the feast of Thanksgiving which is commemorated on the last Thursday of November by the people of the United States at the present time. Thus it was that the annual maturity of the corn in the fields necessitated a period of great industry on the part of our pioneers. Every ear had to be gathered and garnered safely away.

The pioneer family in the United States of America was a relatively self-sustaining unit. Lands for farming had to be cleared by them; they built their houses; they harvested their crops. Very early, however, they learned that families were dependent upon each other in great measure and the role of neighbor was a respected and honored one. When trees were to be felled and brush cleared from a plot of ground, the men and older boys from various families in the vicinity all joined together for the task. When logs were to be split and a cabin built, the job was completed in much shorter time if the father of the family had the help of his neighbors; the term "house raising" was applied to such united building projects. In the same fashion, the men of a particular section, and often the women as well, gathered together to harvest their respective crops of corn. Often, the first part of the week was devoted to one farm and, when that crop was in, the harvesters moved to a neighboring farm to gather the corn from its fields. The last corn to be brought in marked the end of this particular task and was a cause for general celebration.

After the corn had been gathered from the fields, it had to be husked and stored in bins, ready to be fed to stock, to be utilized for the making of hominy, and to be ground up for meal to be used in bread and grits. This called for a second stage of group work—the husking of the corn.

This communal method of working was often called a "bee," perhaps because the corporate industry of the people suggested the work of the bee in making honey. References from accounts of Early America are made to a Quilting Bee, when the women met for the purpose of completing, in a short while, a fancy quilt; this title was also given to the harvesting of corn as one of the most popular of the rural festivals in America from Maine to Florida.[1] It was in the Midwest, however, where vast fields of corn were planted, that the Corn-Husking Bee as an indigenous American festival achieved its greatest development. The Corn-Husking Bee served social as well as economic purposes. When the husking task was completed, the people celebrated the end of the work with feasting, dancing, and contests. The dinners usually featured some types of corn dishes—corn fritters, roasted corn, creamed corn, corn bread, or corn cakes. Walsh also has recorded a custom in which the young men and women began their husking with an eager search for a red ear of corn. The first individual to discover a red ear reigned as king or queen of the festivities which followed the husking.[2] Another custom associated with the husking of a red ear of corn permitted the young man to kiss the girl of his choice.[3]

Dancing or play-party games, to the accompaniment of "fiddles" or the singing voice, constituted the chief form of merrymaking at traditional Corn-Husking Bees; corn-husking contests in which men competed to determine which individual could husk the greatest number of ears of corn in a given time were conducted. In some sections of the country, other contests, based upon activities which were common in the daily work lives of the people, were also held. Such contests included hog calling and chicken calling. The Corn-Husking Bee was

---

[1] William S. Walsh, *Curiosities of Popular Custom* (Philadelphia: J. B. Lippincott Co., 1925), p. 277.
[2] *Ibid.*, p. 277.
[3] *Ibid.*, p. 278.

—and continues to be in the midwestern and southwestern sections of the United States— a colorful celebration characterized by a wholesome spirit of play during well-earned leisure hours.

Production

The Corn-Husking Bee is an authentic folk festival which is especially adaptable to production by school and college or civic groups as a type of festival in which everyone who attends participates. It should be held in the fall of the year, preferably during the latter part of October or early in November. The invitations and posters for publicity should feature decorative themes centered about the activities of the festival with autumnal motifs such as leaves, pumpkins, shocks of corn, *et cetera*. The Bee should be an evening occasion held from 7:00 p.m. until 10:00 p.m.

Site

The ideal site for a Corn-Husking Bee is a large barn. This, however, is seldom available and rarely feasible. A large area with a smooth surface for dancing, either indoors or outdoors, serves very nicely as a place for the Bee. In some sections of the country where the weather permits out-of-doors costumes at this time of year which are not so bundlesome as to preclude dancing, the exhilarating tang to the October nights gives a zest to a Corn-Husking Bee held outside and is considered more enjoyable than an indoor Bee.

Decorations

The site for the Corn-Husking Bee should be decorated to resemble a rustic setting, preferably a large barn in which an original Bee might have been held. Hay, either baled or loose, shocks of corn, and pumpkins lend themselves best for purposes of decoration. A wagon filled with hay, an old well or replica of a windmill and, for out-of-door settings, a rustic, zig-zag rail fence lend atmosphere conducive to the spirit of the occasion. It is desirable to have a fairly large raised platform located on the edge of the dancing area on which the musicians and the folk dance callers may function and on which the finals for the contests may be held so that those attending the festival may have a better view of these particular activities.

Activities

1. *Grand March*

    The Grand March opens the festivities and should be accompanied by spirited American folk tunes which have a good walking tempo. Participants in the festival march in couples. It is advisable to have someone direct the Grand March.

2. *Dancing*

    Dances for the Corn-Husking Bee should be chosen so that everyone may participate; the selection of specific dances to be used, therefore, should be limited to those which are fairly simple so that they may be quickly and easily learned. Suitable dances are *Shoo Fly*, the *Paw Paw Patch*, *Captain Jinks*, the *Oxford Minuet*, *Life on the Ocean Wave*, *The Circle*, and the *American Schottische* and *Polka*.[1] If the group participating is one which is familiar with the basic principles of square dancing, simple square dances may be included, also.

[1] Anne Schley Duggan, *et al*, *Folk Dances of the United States and Mexico* (New York: A. S. Barnes and Company, 1948).

An intermission in the dancing period, in which all participants in the Corn-Husking Bee take part, may serve as a time of rest for the dancers as well as an opportunity for the presentation of special dances by a skilled group of performers. The demonstration set may dance *Grand Square, Ladies to the Center and Back to the Bar*, and *Birdie in a Cage*.[1]

3. *Music and Singing*

Ideal music to accompany the dancing and singing is an instrumental ensemble composed of a violin, an accordion, a guitar, a bass violin and probably a piano to give volume, particularly in an outdoor festival. Group singing of traditional American songs serves as an excellent and satisfying activity and also provides something for the group to do while the judges are determining winners of contests. Songs which are especially well-liked by groups for singing include "Home on the Range," "The Quilting Party," "Oh, Suzanna," "Old Black Joe," "My Bonnie Lies Over the Ocean," "Little Brown Jug," *et cetera*.

As a part of the program during the intermission, individuals, duets, trios, or quartets may present folk songs and ballads as entertainment for those participating in the festival.

4. *Contests*

The contests should be featured in the publicity materials so that a large number of persons enter each one. Preliminary contests should be held on the day preceding the festival so that there are three, or possibly five, finalists in each event on the night of the Corn-Husking Bee itself.

While the basis for entering specific contests may be strictly individual, the spirit of competition may be heightened when eligibility comprises entrants representative of various units of organization within a school, college, or community. For example, in a high school situation, entrance might be made on the basis of home rooms; in colleges, units of competition might be based upon dormitories, fraternities and sororities, or college classifications; in community situations, the basis might be church groups, club groups, neighborhoods, or streets.

a. Hog-Calling and *Chicken-Calling Contests*.

Contestants compete, one at a time, in the "art" of calling hogs and chickens. The contests are staged separately and those who enter one may or may not enter another.

b. Costume Contest.

The costume contest may be conducted during the Grand March. Judges may screen the group as they march around for the ten most appropriate costumes. Appropriateness of costume depends upon how closely and effectively the couples have reproduced the type of dress suitable for a rural party during pioneer days. These ten couples should be notified that they are to appear in the finals when they march around the platform so that the judges may select the winners.

---

[1]Duggan, *et al, op. cit.*

c. *Husband-Calling Contest.*

Although this contest has no definite authentic origin in the Corn-Husking Bees of our pioneers, it represents a part of their daily lives as wives called husbands in from the barns and fields to their meals. In recent years, therefore, it has been added as one of the Corn-Husking Bee activities conducted in various sections of the Southwest.

d. *Dance Contests.*

Sets of dancers may compete in square dance contests or couples may compete in round dances, such as the polka, varsovienne, schottische, and waltz. The best dancers should be chosen from each of the square and round dance categories.

e. *Corn-Husking Contest.*

Bushels of corn should be allocated to each individual or couple—making a team—who are competing in this particular event of the Bee. At a given signal, they begin to husk the corn and continue until a signal to stop is given when the ears are counted and the individual or team with the greatest number of husked ears is proclaimed the winner. This particular contest can prove an untidy one and usually leaves the floor strewn with husks unless the necessary precautions are taken against this contingency. One expedient precaution is the spreading of a tarpaulin over the area needed for the contest which can be folded up, husks inside, and removed to leave a clean floor. Huskers place the clean ears in the baskets so that they may be counted more readily.

f. *Group Singing.*

Various groups compete in singing authentic American folk songs which may be arranged as the group wishes to present them. Elaborate song presentations which do not have a folk quality should be discouraged.

Judges for the contest finals should be seated so that they face the platform. The group attending the festival may seat themselves or stand about the platform. Suitable prizes should be awarded to those winning first and second places in each of the contests conducted. Suggested prizes are fried chicken and candy corn for the chicken-calling contest, a picnic ham or a baby pig and a ham sandwich or a piggy bank for the hog-calling contest, a box of candy and candy corn for the corn-husking contest, a cake and jelly beans or cookies for the costume contest, a cake and a bag of apples for the sing-song contest, and an album of square dance tunes or early American folk music and a folk song book for the dance contest.

Suggested Schedule of Activities for The Corn-Husking Bee

Grand March _____ 7:00
Dancing _____ 7:15
    Paw Paw Patch   *Captain Jinks*
    Shoo Fly   *Oxford Minuet*
Intermission with Program _____ 7:45
    Dances by Demonstration Set:
    Ladies to the Center and Back to the Bar   *Birdie in a Cage*
                  Grand Square

Songs by Special Performers:
"Bonnie Barbara Allen"   "On Springfield Mountain"
                    "The Old Chisholm Trail"

Dancing _____ 8:15
   American Schottische   *Life on the Ocean Wave*
                 The Circle

Contests _____ 8:45
   Chicken-Calling   Husband-Calling
   Hog-Calling   Square and Round Dance
   Costume   Corn-Husking

Group Singing _____ 9:30
Announcement of Contest Winners _____ 9:45

5. *Refreshments*

Typical and suitable refreshments are hot cider, milk, hot corn sticks, doughnuts, apples, popcorn, and roasted peanuts which may be served from a table.

An English May Day Festival

The celebration of the first of May, or May Day, in the British Isles had its origin in both the Druidic rites of the early Celts in the northern sections of the islands—Ireland, Scotland and Northern England—and in the pagan Roman *Floralia* introduced to the Anglo-Saxons of Southern England at the time of the Roman invasion of these countries. The Celtic May Day rites were celebrated in honor of the sun god, Bel, and were observed with bonfires and with animal sacrifices. The Anglo-Saxon observances of May Day had their origin in the Roman Floral Games celebrated in honor of the goddess, Flora, and were expressed in the form of a flower festival. Walsh traces the May Day festivals back to the still more ancient phallic festivals of India and Egypt which used a pole, like the Maypole, as a symbol of fertility and were celebrated at the season of the year when new life appeared in field and woods.[1] Because of the nature of the English celebration of May Day, however, authorities believe that the festival in that particular country was derived most directly from the Roman *Floralia*. The use of flowers to decorate houses, to adorn animals, and to festoon the Maypole link the ancestry of this particular English celebration more directly to a flower festival than to one entailing animal sacrifice.[2] In Scotland, Ireland, and in some sections of Northern England, however, vestiges of the Druidic celebration of May Day are still observed and some of its elements have been incorporated into the traditional May Day festivals of England.

The May Day festival reached its peak of popularity during Medieval and Tudor England —a popularity which continued to the period of the Reformation. During this time, it achieved eminence as one of the chief public holidays and was observed by all of the people of Eng-

[1]Walsh, *op. cit.*, p. 682.
[2]*Ibid.*, p. 683.

land regardless of their social or economic status. The celebration began with expeditions to the woods to gather boughs and flowers which were used to decorate houses, shops, and even the heads of horses and cattle, and the most important item of all—the tree to serve as the Maypole itself. These trips into the forests were usually undertaken by the youth of each village and were made either the previous evening or in the early hours of the May Day morning.[1] In any case, at sun-up the May Day festivities began. The Maypole was decorated with flowers and ribbons and set up in the center of the village or in an equally prominent place, often upon the village green. At times, the Maypole was painted prior to its erection, usually in spiral lines of two contrasting colors; yellow and black and green and white are both recorded as colors often chosen.

The events of the day included the crowning of a May Queen, dancing, and competitive sports and games with archery a particularly popular activity in which yeomen shot for fat purses, their markmanship admired and cheered by the crowd. The highlight of the day was the arrival of Robin Hood and his friends and the accompanying Morris dancers and their accessory figures. Robin Hood usually served as Lord of the May and Maid Marian as his Lady.[2] To the English people, Robin Hood, as he was perpetuated in legend, constituted the symbol of the common man—brave, adventurous, honest, a protector of women, devout, and devoted to the virtuous life yet fun-loving, light-hearted and fond of the free, out-of-door life.[3] Early in the history of May Day celebrations, the Maid Marian was a man in woman's attire and at one time was one of the figures associated with the Morris dancers. A Fool accompanied Robin Hood to provide fun and amusement for the crowd with his antics. Friar Tuck was, according to legend, the chaplain affiliated with Robin Hood's band.

Usually, Robin Hood, Little John, and Robin Hood's men are depicted dressed in the garb of yeomen of Medieval England consisting of coat, hood, and hose, and carrying bows and arrows. Their costume is described most often as green in color, probably because, as the legend goes, they lived in Sherwood Forest near the village of Nottingham.[4] Maid Marian's costume is depicted as that of the fifteenth century dress of ladies of noble rank, including a tall pointed hat draped with a flowing veil, a tight laced bodice and a long skirt with a pannier.[5]

The traditional costume of the Fool included a hood decorated with asses' ears and with a crest resembling a cockscomb, a doublet, tight hose of contrasting colors on either leg, and slippers with long, pointed, upturned toes. His costume had bells hanging from it and he carried a ridiculous staff.[6] The colors which predominated in the Fool's costume were red, yellow, and blue.[7]

---

[1]John Brand, *Observations on Popular Antiquities* (London: Chatto and Windus, Picadilly, 1877), p. 117.
[2]Walsh, *op. cit.*, p. 683.
[3]*Encyclopaedia Britannica*, 14th ed., Vol. 19 (Chicago: Encyclopaedia Britannica, 1939), p. 350.
[4]*Ibid.*
[5]Jeannette Lincoln, *The Festival Book* (New York: A. S. Barnes Company, 1929), p. 70.
[6]*Encyclopaedia Britannica*, *op. cit.*, Vol. 9, p. 467.
[7]Brand, *op. cit.*, p. 147.

Friar Tuck is represented in an old English stained glass window as one of a mendicant order in a russet clerical habit, a red and gold corded girdle, and red stockings. He carries in his hand a chaplet of red and white beads and wears a wallet hanging from his girdle.[1]

The Morris dancers dressed in white and wore bells of different tones so that the sound when they danced resulted in a harmony of bells.[2] The Hobby Horse and the Jack-in-the-Green were accessory figures to the Morris dancers. The horse itself is depicted in the window mentioned above as being of a reddish-white color ''like the beautiful blossom of the peach-tree.'' The man carrying the Hobby Horse wears a doublet of two colors — red on the left side and yellow on the right.[3] The Jack-in-the-Green is a man encased from the hips up in a cone-shaped framework some ten feet high which is decorated with green boughs and flowers and provides a peep-hole at eye level.[4]

Throughout the day, the general populace danced, paid homage to the May Queen, participated in games and partook of festal foods which included, traditionally, a form of syllabub made from warm cow's milk, cake, and wine.[5] Toward evening, they watched stage plays and built bonfires.[6]

In later years, the celebration of the May Day was carried on primarily by the milkmaids who decorated themselves and their cows with flowers and drove them through the streets as they called upon their customers,[7] and still later by the chimney sweeps, who blackened their faces and danced through the streets dressed in ''tawdry finery.'' In London, the first of May is known today as Sweeps' Day.

One May Day custom which is still observed in some sections of England is practiced by young girls and consists of washing their faces in the early morning dew in order to insure twelve months of rosy cheeks, and of bathing their faces in the dew on the hawthorne tree early on May Day morning to promote greater comeliness.[8]

Production

The English May Day celebration lends itself especially to a reproduction in schools and colleges or by civic groups as a re-enactment of an authentic festival for educational purposes. This type of festival serves as a culminating project or activity with which to conclude a unit on the study of English folk dance. Ideally, an English May Day festival should be held on May first according to the original English custom; if that date is not convenient, however, it is possible to celebrate this festival on some other day in May since records indicate an extension of the games and dances commemorating this occasion over a period of several days during the month of May.[9]

---

[1] Brand, *op. cit.*, p. 146.

[2] *Encyclopaedia Britannica*, 14th ed., Vol. 15 (Chicago: Encyclopaedia Britannica, Inc., 1939).

[3] Brand, *op. cit.*, p. 150.

[4] Joseph Strutt, *The Sports and Pastimes of the People of England* (London: Thomas Tegg, 73, Cheapside, 1838), p. 358.

[5] Brand, *op. cit.*, p. 124.

[6] Strutt, *op. cit.*, p. 351.

[7] Robert Chambers, *The Book of Days*, Vol. I (Philadelphia: J. B. Lippincott Co., 1864), p. 573.

[8] Walsh, *op. cit.*, p. 868.

[9] Strutt, *op. cit.*, p. 355.

An ideal site for the production of an English May Day Festival is the grassy area of an athletic field or any expanse of smooth, grassy surface comparable to the village greens upon which this traditional festival was first held. While the original festival lasted throughout the day, it is justifiable to condense its re-enactment into an event of one or two hours' duration, preferably in the late afternoon before sundown. Invitations and publicity announcing the festival should be designed to convey a suggestion of the spirit of the festival and may be worded in Middle English and perhaps written in English script of this particular period. Decorations should center about the Maypole which should be gaily crowned with flowers and colored streamers.[1] Other decorations might include an old rustic well, the bower with the throne where the May Queen and her attendants sit, a replica of the stocks used for punishing petty misdemeanors of the given period, and several poles to be greased and used in the contests planned. Tables with refreshments of cakes, tea, and milk should be placed in convenient spots and decorated with greenery and flowers appropriate to the occasion.

Those who are participating in the festival other than the central characters should be costumed in the dress of village folk of the early part of the seventeenth century.

Activities

1. *Entrance of Robin Hood and his men with Maid Marian.*

    Robin Hood and his men—including Little John and several yeomen, Friar Tuck, the Fool, and Maid Marian—enter the festival grounds. Robin Hood is the hero of the occasion and the people select him to serve as Lord of the May. In planning a festival, further interest may be stimulated if Robin Hood, Maid Marian, and the May Queen are elected by popular vote from among the group to participate in the celebration. Little John and the men to accompany Robin Hood should be chosen on the basis of their skill in archery since Robin Hood's men particularly are expected to enter and to win the archery contests. The Fool should be some small, agile person capable of carrying on in an amusing fashion the antics of the Fool such as an occasional cartwheel or handspring.

2. *Crowning of the May Queen.*

    The May Queen and her attendants—two or four in number—should be dressed in white and should wear flowers in their hair. Robin Hood, as Lord of the May, crowns the Queen. She should sit on a throne in an especially constructed bower decorated with greenery, and her attendants should seat themselves about her throne. The crown should be one made of flowers. The May Queen and her attendants reign over the festivities and participate only with smiles, gracious countenances, and other means of applause of the activities presented in their honor.

3. *Maypole Dance*

    There are no absolutely authentic Maypole dances recorded as such for reproduction in conjunction with an English May Day festival. The single factor in every Maypole dance which is truly authentic is the weaving of colored streamers at the conclusion of the dance so that the top section of the pole is sheathed in a bright, plaited design.

---

[1]Detailed directions for decorating a Maypole are given in Lincoln, *op. cit.*, p. 65.

91

Traditional colors for Maypole streamers include bright blue, green, yellow, orange, pink, and violet. The actual weaving is usually preceded by a dance. For this particular May Day Festival, the authors suggest *Sellenger's Round*[1] because it is an authentic English country dance performed in circular formation by any number of couples and a smooth transition may be made from this dance to the weaving of the streamers about the Maypole itself. The following procedure for winding the Maypole is recommended as a simple, effective one in keeping with the spirit of an English May Day festival: At the conclusion of *Sellenger's Round*, the dancers form a single circle, facing in. In unison, the women go in to the Maypole, take hold of their streamers and return to their places; the men then do the same. Holding their respective streamers fairly taut so that a neat design may be effected upon the pole, the dancers turn to form a single circle with partners facing, and dance a grand right and left, using the English running or skipping step. The weaving of streamers down the Maypole is achieved as the men pass their streamers under those of their respective partners, then over the streamers of the women they meet next — the women passing first over and then under — and continue this alternation of under and over with the streamers until the Maypole has been wound down to within one-fourth or one-third of the distance from the top, depending upon the height of the pole. If continued too long, the winding can become monotonous for spectators and exhausting for participants. When the weaving is completed, dancers should release their streamers and run or skip back to their places in the crowd.

4. *Dancing by the people.*

Dancers should know exactly how they are to be arranged in groups and spaced on the dancing area for each of the dances scheduled and should be rehearsed carefully in the cues which tell them when to form these groups for general participation in the country dances selected as well as when and how to respond to other cues with which the activities of the festival as a whole are woven together. Dances to be included are: *Rufty Tufty, Row Well, Ye Mariners, The Black Nag,* and *Gathering Peascods,* all of which may be found in *Folk Dances of the British Isles.*[2]

5. *Contests.*

 a. *Archery.*

Targets should be placed in such a way that all safety precautions may be observed in setting up the range and that spectators may see as well. Those entering the competition compete for a purse which should be of a drawstring, pouch type containing silver coins. The target may be a replica of a cock set upon a post. The archer who shoots nearest the heart of the cock wins the purse.

 b. *Races.*

Races which have an authentic origin for use in traditional English May Day festivals are foot-races — which involve simple running; stilt races — which are competitive events on stilts; and sack races — in which contestants step into sturdy burlap sacks,

[1]Cecil J. Sharp, *The Country Dance Book*, Part IV (London: Novello and Company, Ltd., 1916), p. 40.
[2]Anne Schley Duggan, *et al*, *Folk Dances of the British Isles* (New York: A. S. Barnes and Company, 1948).

holding the open end of the sacks up about their hips, and jump along or progress in the fastest manner possible, staying within the sacks into which they have stepped. Any one or all three of these races may be used. The contestants line up, Robin Hood giving the signal for them to start by lowering his hand and shouting "Go!" The people cheer during each race and acclaim the winner with cries of "Hurrah!"

c. *Climbing the greased pole.*

One or more sturdy, smooth poles—twelve to fifteen feet in height—should be erected, each supporting suitable prizes at the top. The poles are greased and, at a given signal, the contestants, preferably small boys from ten to twelve years of age, begin to climb. Each contestant climbs until he captures a prize from the top of his pole which may be a knife or some similar object of value to a boy of his age.

6. *Entrance of the Morris Dancers and the presentation of a stick Morris dance and a handkerchief Morris dance.*

The Morris dancers should be accompanied by musicians, the Hobby Horse, the Jack-in-the-Green, and any other accessory figures desired (See account of Morris dancers in *Folk Dances of the British Isles.*[1]). The dancers enter with the *Tideswell Processional*[2] and present *Bean-Setting* and *Blue-Eyed Stranger.*[3]

7. *Presentation of a play by the actors.*

The actors, in costume, present "Pyramus and Thisbe" from Act V of Shakespeare's *Midsummer-Night's Dream.* The brief, humorous play may be produced without the aid of scenery but may be heightened in humor if the actors have props which suggest their respective characterizations. The Department of Speech or Drama should be consulted in the details of the presentation of the play and it is highly desirable that they assume responsibility for its authentic preparation and production. At the conclusion of the play, three of the dancers present *Wyresdale Greensleeves.*[4]

8. *Singing*

The group of village folk presents old English folk songs which have been practiced prior to the festival. If possible, someone from the Department of Music should select authentic English songs which were sung during this particular period in England and should teach the group to sing them properly.

Script

The people in attendance at the festival are milling about the village green in a holiday mood, chatting with friends and greeting acquaintances. A few of the men are engaged in

---

[1]Duggan, *et al, op. cit.*

[2]Cecil J. Sharp and Herbert C. Macilwaine, *The Morris Book*, 2nd ed., Part I (London: Novello and Company, Ltd., 1912), p. 118.

[3]Duggan, *et al., op. cit.*

[4]Cecil J. Sharp and George Butterworth. *The Morris Book*, Part V (London: Novello and Company, Ltd., 1913), p. 111.

bowling on the green. Some of the children are chasing each other in impromptu games of tag; others are watching the Village Fool cutting capers. His antics attract a group of the adults and soon he is the center of a crowd rocking with boisterous laughter. Suddenly, eight of the town soldiers appear, seize the Fool, and place him in stocks. The people protest this action by recoiling from the soldiers, traditional enemies of their popular hero, Robin Hood, into mumbling, grumbling groups from which such cries resound as

"Leave him alone!"

"He's done no harm!"

"You've spoiled the fun!"

The soldiers leave amid the disgruntled mutterings of the crowd and immediately the blast of a horn is heard in the distance. Someone shouts

"It is the horn of Robin Hood!"

Others cry

"Hurrah! Here come Robin Hood and his jolly men!"

"Robin Hood shall be the Lord of the May!"

Robin Hood, Maid Marian, Friar Tuck, the Fool, Little John, and Robin Hood's men run onto the festival area amid hearty shouts and cries of welcome. Robin Hood frees the Village Fool from the stocks and then, turning to the crowd, says gaily

"Greetings, good folk, 'Tis the first of May—

Which gentle maid reigns as Queen this day?"

He is answered with cries of

"Pretty Betty Brown"[1]

"Here she comes with her ladies!"

A man in the crowd cries

"Who shall crown the Queen this year?"

Everyone shouts

"Robin Hood!" "Robin Hood!"

Robin Hood meets the Queen and escorts her to the throne where he places the crown of flowers on her head. He steps down and bows to her, turns to the people, and cries

"As a toast to our Queen,

We'll wind the honored Maypole—

Make way for the Maypole dancers!"

When the Maypole is finished, Robin Hood turns to the people and cries

"And now—

A dance on the Green

In honor of our Queen!"

Village folk take places and dance *Rufty Tufty* and *The Black Nag*, effecting their exchange in formations for the two dances quickly. Large numbers of participants may utilize the dance

---

[1]The name of the May Queen elected to reign in each specific situation in which the festival is presented should be substituted for that of "Betty Brown" given here.

area most effectively by having the two couples comprising each set for *Rufty Tufty* face in alternate directions. Such an arrangement of sets will also yield extraordinary beauty of design for the dancing of the group as a whole provided the individual sets are carefully spaced upon the dancing area. The longways sets for *The Black Nag* should face the area set aside for spectators with Robin Hood and Maid Marian, as Lord and Lady of the May Day, respectively, in the foreground.

When the dancing is over and the dancers are resting, someone from the crowd cries
"Let's have the contests!"
Others join in with cries of
"Yes, the contests!"
"The archery first!"
At this point, the Archery Contest is held. The people applaud good shots and acclaim the winner. Then someone cries
"What of the races!
Let's have the races!"
The contests continue with the Foot Race, the Stilt Race, and the Sack Race. Someone shouts
"Where are the lads to climb the poles?
Let's see them reach the prizes!"
The Greased Pole Climbing Contest follows.

As the shouts from the crowd die down after the last boy has reached his prize, the tinkling of bells is heard in the distance and someone in the crowd cries
"Listen to the bells,
The Morris dancers are coming!"
Morris dancers, accompanied by accessory figures, enter with the *Tideswell Processional* and then dance *Bean-Setting* and *Blue-Eyed Stranger* in established places upon the dancing area.

When they finish, there is much applause and someone cries
"Where are the actors?
A play, a play!"
The actors are brought out of the crowd and present "Pyramus and Thisbe." At the close of the play, Pyramus rises and says, "Will it please you to hear an epilogue, or to see a dance?" The people shout "A dance, a dance!" Three of the actors dance *Wyresdale Greensleeves*.

At the close of the dance, Robin Hood cries
"Let's dance to the day
Ere the sun fades away!"
The people take their places and dance *Row Well, Ye Mariners* and *Gathering Peascods*.

When the dances are over, the people gather around the May Queen's bower and sing. After a few songs, the May Queen rises to leave. Robin Hood and his company go first to escort her to her home, the Queen follows with her attendants, and the people come after, singing "Summer is A-Coming In." The festival is over.

A Mexican Folk Dance Party—*Noche Mexicana*

This *Noche Mexicana*—Mexican Evening—is suggested as a folk dance party based upon typical Mexican party customs. Its purpose is to enable those who attend and participate to experience social activities—dances, songs, games, and feasting—from Mexico in the type of setting in which the people of that country enjoy such activities. Those included in the planning of this particular party, therefore, are typical of the activities in which the Mexican people engage in their social play.

Production

The *Noche Mexicana* should be held in the evening and, to be truly Mexican in character, should be scheduled from nine o'clock until midnight. The invitations and publicity might feature the *china poblana* and *charro* who dance the *Jarabe Tapatío*, a Mexican hat and *sarape*, a gay *piñata* in the shape of an animal, ship, or fowl, or any other suitable Mexican motif.

Site

The site for the *Noche Mexicana* should be any large area with a surface suitable for dancing representative of the traditional plaza of every Mexican village which serves as a gathering place for social activities. For an out-of-doors party, a section of a broad, paved street, a cement tennis court, a paved quadrangle, or any other expansive smooth surface may be used. An indoor party may be held in a gymnasium, a ballroom, or any similar inside area.

Decorations

Around the edges of the area, booths or stalls should be erected with counters from across which food may be served. The center of this area should be reserved for dancing with tables and chairs surrounding it, allowing sufficient space between the tables and the booths for the comfortable passage of participants. If the party is held indoors, *piñatas* may be hung from the ceiling over the dancing area; if it is an out-of-doors party, they may be suspended from ropes or cords which span the dancing area. In any case, they should be far enough apart and of a sufficient number to allow approximately one *piñata* to every twenty-five individuals attending the party. The tables should be covered with colored cloths, either solid or striped, and each table should have a large candle in its center. Further decoration may be achieved by large imitation cacti cut out of cardboard, painted, and then set conveniently and artistically about the site established for this particular folk dance party. Colorful Mexican *sarapes* and blankets may be hung from the booths for added atmosphere.

Costumes

The spirit of participation on the part of those attending this illustrative Mexican folk dance party may be heightened and a great deal added to the color and atmosphere of the party itself if guests wear costumes which, if not truly authentic, are, at least, suggestive of traditional Mexican party clothes. In large Mexican cities, of course, the party dress of men and women is the tuxedo and evening gown, respectively—the formal dress found in any large metropolitan city. The real fiesta dress for the Mexican man, however, is the *charro* suit. If such a costume is not available, men wishing to attend the *Noche Mexicana* in costume may wear white or dark slacks, a white sports shirt, a solid colored scarf[1] worn under the collar and tied in a square knot at the neck, and a large-brimmed, light-colored straw or felt hat. Women may wear either long or calf-length full, gaily colored skirts of plain or printed fabrics which are gathered at the waist, white short-sleeved, peasant blouses, and *huaraches* or sandals. They may either plait their hair with colored ribbons intertwined within the plaits or wear vivid flowers over each ear or in the form of a coronet.

Food

The food should be served from the booths outlining the site chosen for the celebration of the *Noche Mexicana*. Those in charge of dispensing food and beverages from the various booths should be dressed in the appropriate costumes described for the Mexican men and women of the working classes in *Folk Dances of the United States and Mexico*.[2]

Those who are participating in the party, should procure their own food from the various booths and take it to their respective tables; waiters or waitresses in costumes may remove dishes from each table when those seated have finished eating and drinking.

There should be enough tables and chairs to accommodate all who plan to attend the Mexican folk dance party. Since the food to be served is a very important part of the *Noche Mexicana*, some fee will have to be charged to all who come unless the group sponsoring the party has a budget commensurate with the expenditures involved. The financial problem might be solved by having each person pay at each booth for the food purchased; a more expedient and convenient plan, however, is to have each person attending the *Noche Mexicana* reserve a place at a table and pay a fee for this reservation. In this way, the Foods Committee can estimate more accurately the amount of food to prepare.

There may be several booths, depending upon the size of the crowd, which serve tamales, enchiladas, chili, tortillas, and tacos.[3] Another booth may serve sliced canteloupe and water-melon (if they are in season and therefore obtainable), bananas, pineapple, oranges, grapes, and mangos. Another booth should serve coffee and hot chocolate. An Indian woman with a charcoal stove may serve hot, boiled corn on the cob from a kettle. Another woman may sell candy—the burnt caramel type—from a small glass case on a table or from the top of the table. A man with a suitable cart may sell ice cream and frozen suckers. Several men and women in costume may carry baskets of eggs filled with confetti to pass out to the guests. In preparing these, the egg itself is blown out so that the shell remains intact before being

---

[1]Typical colors are bright red, green, orange, or purple.

[2]Anne Schley Duggan, *et al, Folk Dances of the United States and Mexico* (New York: A. S. Barnes and Company, 1948).

[3]Tortillas, which form the basis for enchiladas and tacos, are difficult to prepare and should be purchased in cans. Tamales may be purchased in cans, also. The ingredients and directions for preparing chili, enchiladas, and tacos may be obtained from grocery stores which handle Mexican foods.

filled with confetti and broken over the heads of friends or thrown at various individuals to shower them with confetti.

Music

Music is an important aspect of a *Noche Mexicana* and functions in one capacity or another from the beginning to the end of the party. For the dancing and accompaniment to *El Jarabe Tapatío*, the ideal form of music is a typical Mexican orchestra, in costume, composed of violins, cornet, trombone, drums and other percussion instruments such as gourds, rattles, and sticks. In many situations, it might prove a stupendous task indeed for a group of musicians to learn all of the music suggested for the *Noche Mexicana* although the use of such an orchestra lends immeasurably to the color and atmosphere of the occasion. A second best alternative is the use of records of the recommended music which have been made by Mexican orchestras and which may be purchased from any one of several large record companies.

Activities

1. *Paseo*

The party begins with a *paseo* in which the men and women walk around the dancing area, the men, on the outside, moving in a clockwise direction and the women, on the inside, moving in a counterclockwise direction. They may not maintain a definite circular formation but move in the general directions indicated. The *paseo* is accompanied by music, usually marches, *pasos dobles*, or any suitable semi-classic or classic selections. In Mexico, young people do not have "dates," as such. A young girl goes down to the plaza on Sunday evenings or to the *Alameda*, or park, on Sunday mornings with her family or with a group of her friends and participates in the *paseo*. After a few trips around the circle, a young man usually asks her to join him and she walks with him in the direction in which he is moving. They talk and walk for a while and then go over to a bench to chat and listen to the music. When the music stops and the *paseo* is over, the girl rejoins her family or friends and goes home. In adapting the *paseo* to the *Noche Mexicana*, outlined as a typical Mexican folk dance party in this chapter of *The Teaching of Folk Dance*, couples may separate to begin the *paseo* following which each man may invite his partner to walk with him after one or two revolutions around the circle. When all of the couples meet again, they may break away from the *paseo* to begin the period devoted to social dancing.

2. *Dancing*

The general period of dancing begins after the *paseo*. Music for dancing should be selected from Mexican folk songs of the *ranchero* type. A collection of these tunes, which includes waltzes as well as selections written in duple meter, may be purchased in Mexico.[1] The dancing time is interspersed with a special floor show. At the close of the first half of the dancing period, a demonstration group may teach *La Virgencita*[2], a delightful

[1] *15 Exitos Rancheros Mexicanos* (Mexico, D.F.: Promotora Hispana Americana de Musica, S.A.).
[2] Duggan, *et al, op. cit.*

Mexican folk dance, to the guests participating in the party. At the close of the latter part of the dancing period, the same group may teach *La Jesucita*[1] so that all may enjoy this simple Mexican folk dance.

3. *Floor Show*

The floor show begins with a group of young girls in the costume of the women of Tehuantepec[2] carrying trays filled with flowers or fruit who sing "La Sandunga." When they leave, four little old men enter in costumes[3] and dance *Los Viejitos*.[4] As they exit, singers—preferably with a guitar for accompaniment—come in and sing "Jalisco" and "¡Viva Mexico!" The crowd may join in to shout the "*vivas*" in the latter song. These singers move off and soldiers come in to sing some of the *corridos* from the revolutionary days. Those suggested are "Adelita" and "La Cucaracha." While they are singing, a group of girls enter and stand to the side, flirting very subtly with the soldiers. After singing "La Cucaracha," the soldiers invite them to dance and they dance *La Cucaracha*.[5] This completes the floor show and couples participating in the folk dance party return to the social dance activities.

4. *Special closing events.*

The last events of the *Noche Mexicana* are the breaking of the *piñatas* and the dancing of the *Jarabe Tapatío*. For breaking the *piñatas*, individuals gather around the *piñata* nearest their respective tables. By prearrangement, one person should be in charge of each *piñata*. In every group, one person is blindfolded, given a stick, turned around three times and given three tries with the stick to hit the *piñata*. If he or she is unsuccessful after the third try, another is blindfolded and so on until the *piñata* is broken when all scramble for the nuts and candies contained therein which shower down onto the floor. A space is cleared and the *china poblana* and the *charro*, in costume, dance the *Jarabe Tapatío*.[6] The audience cheers them in the *diana* and the performers take the final position of the dance amid bursts of applause to bring to a close the *Noche Mexicana*.

Program

In order that the *Noche Mexicana* may have more meaning for those who attend without the awkward procedure of having someone explain the various parts of the party, the authors suggest a program to be given to the guests, as they come in the door or entrance to the party site, which will prove both informative and attractive. A suggested type of such a program is given below:

PROGRAM

¡*Saludos, Amigos*! The *Noche Mexicana* is planned to afford you a few hours of the kind of social entertainment enjoyed by our neighbors "South of the Border." ¡*Bienvenidos Todos*!

---

[1]Mary Effie Shambaugh, *Folk Festivals* (New York: A. S. Barnes and Company, 1932), p. 50.
[2]Frances Toor, *A Treasury of Mexican Folkways* (New York: Crown Publishers, 1947), p. 79.
[3]See costume depicted on the Mexican Costume Plate in *Folk Dances of the United States and Mexico*.
[4]Duggan, *et al., op. cit.*
[5]*Ibid*
[6]*Ibid.*

Dinner _ 9:00 – 10:00

Menu

Tamales, enchiladas, chili, tacos

Corn on the cob   Tortillas

Fruit – Candy – Ice Cream

Coffee   Chocolate

Paseo _ 10:00 – 10:15

After dinner, guests are invited to join the *paseo* in the center of the floor. According to an old Mexican custom, women walk around counterclockwise on the inside of a circle while men walk clockwise on the outside of such a circle. After a few trips around, each man invites his partner to walk with him and they chat, continuing in the direction in which the men are walking. When all couples are together again, they may break away from the *paseo* and dance.

Dancing _ 10:15 – 11:00

Music played for dancing consists of *ranchero* tunes, a type of folk music from rural sections of Mexico. The final dance before the intermission for the floor show will be *La Virgencita*, a simple Mexican folk dance in two parts. A demonstration group will dance *La Virgencita* and all are invited to join in as soon as they have learned the basic steps.

Floor Show _ _ _ _ _ _ _ _ _ _ _ _ _ _ _ _ _ _ 11:00 – 11:20

"La Sandunga"

A lovely song from the Isthmus of Tehuantepec in the southern part of Mexico. The beautiful, sensuous song has conflicting origins. One attributes the song to the lament of a young man who, when told his mother was dying, hurried on horseback to her bedside, but arrived too late. Another says it originated as friends consoled a young girl forsaken by her lover.

Los Viejitos

A dance from Michoacán in the southwestern part of Mexico, "The Little Old Men," is enjoyed by the Mexicans as one of their most humorous dances. The bent, seemingly wrinkled and senile bodies of the dancers are in reality those of the young, agile men of the particular village in which it is performed. The dance is thought to have a religious origin because of the cross which is described in the floor pattern of some of the figures; it is danced in Mexico today, however, for various secular occasions and is, therefore, an appropriate number in the floor show for a typical social gathering designated as *Noche Mexicana*.

Mexican Songs

"*Jalisco*"
"*¡Viva Mexico!*"
Both of these songs are popular in Mexico today and are sung or played at almost every social gathering. In the chorus of the second song, the members of audiences in Mexico delight in adding a lusty "*viva*" each time after the "*¡Viva Mexico!*" is sung.

Revolutionary Songs and Dance

"*Adelita*"
"*La Cucaracha*"
Mexican soldiers sang these songs in their camps and on marches during the revolution. "Adelita," from the state of Durango, is a ballad relating the story of a young Mexican girl who followed the camps of the troops because she was in love with one of the soldiers. "La Cucaracha," from the state of Chihuahua, is a humorous song with endless verses which soldiers improvised as they sang. The chorus tells of a cockroach who is unable to walk because it has no marihuana to smoke.

Dancing _11:20 – 11:45

The last dance will be a Mexican folk dance, *La Jesucita*. All are invited to participate in this simple dance which the demonstration group will present.

101

Piñata _ 11:45 – 11:55

This charming Mexican custom is an important part of Mexican celebrations, especially those celebrated during the Christmas season as well as in the commemoration of birthdays for specific individuals in this country. For the breaking of the *piñata*, each person should join the group under the *piñata* nearest his table.

El Jarabe Tapatío _ _ _ _ _ _ _ _ _ _ _ _ _ _ _ 11:55 – 12:00

The national dance of Mexico is performed by the *china poblana* and the *charro* and is a part of almost all Mexican celebrations. The Mexican people cheer the dancers in the *diana*, or finale, as they approach the finish of the dance.

ADIÓS

APPENDIX

TABLE OF CONTENTS
for other volumes of
THE FOLK DANCE LIBRARY

Folk Dances of Scandinavia

Folk Dances of European Countries

Folk Dances of the British Isles

English, Scotch, and Irish Costume Plate
Preface
Introduction
- Explanation of Terms, Counting, Music, and Diagrams
- Analysis of Basic Steps, Figures, Terms, Positions, and Formations
- Pronunciation of Foreign Words

Presentation of English, Scottish, and Irish Folk Dances

Map of England, Scotland, and Ireland
Geographical Background
Historical and Sociological Background
Folk Dances
Folk Costumes
Folk Festivals

Analysis of Folk Dances

England:

Rufty Tufty
The Black Nag
Gathering Peascods
Row Well, Ye Mariners
Hunsdon House
Bean-Setting
Blue-Eyed Stranger
Sleights Sword Dance

Scotland:

Highland Schottische
Highland Fling

Ireland:

Irish Long Dance
Irish Lilt

Bibliography

Folk Dances of the United States and Mexico

ALPHABETICAL LIST OF DANCES
IN
THE FOLK DANCE LIBRARY

Dance	*Country*	*Volume*
American Polka	America	*Folk Dances of the United States and Mexico*
American Schottische	America	*"*
American Varsovienne	America	*"*
Bean-Setting	England	*Folk Dances of the British Isles*
Birdie in a Cage	America	*Folk Dances of the United States and Mexico*
Black Nag, The	England	*Folk Dances of the British Isles*
Blue-Eyed Stranger	England	*"*
Branle Gascon	France	*Folk Dances of European Countries*
Boudigueste, La	France	*"*
Circle, The	America	*Folk Dances of the United States and Mexico*
Come, Let Us Be Joyful	Germany	*Folk Dances of European Countries*
Crested Hen, The	Denmark	*Folk Dances of Scandinavia*
Csárdás	Hungary	*Folk Dances of European Countries*
Csébogar	Hungary	*"*
Cucaracha, La	Mexico	*Folk Dances of the United States and Mexico*
Danish Masquerade	Denmark	*Folk Dances of Scandinavia*
Danish Minuet	Denmark	*"*
Danish Schottische	Denmark	*"*
Danish Varsovienne	Denmark	*"*
Feiar	Norway	*"*
Finnish Polka	Finland	*"*
Finnish Schottische	Finland	*"*
Foot Swinging Dance	Germany	*Folk Dances of European Countries*
Four Steps	Czechoslovakia	*"*
Gathering Peascods	England	*Folk Dances of the British Isles*
Gavotte de Guéméné	France	*Folk Dances of European Countries*
Gavotte de Pont-Aven	France	*"*
Gavotte de Quimper	France	*"*

Dance	*Country*	*Volume*
Grand Square	America	*Folk Dances of the United States and Mexico*
Gustaf's Skoal	Sweden	*Folk Dances of Scandinavia*
Hambo	Sweden	''
Handkerchief Dance	Moravia	*Folk Dances of European Countries*
Highland Fling	Scotland	*Folk Dances of the British Isles*
Highland Schottische	Scotland	''
Hull's Victory	America	*Folk Dances of the United States and Mexico*
Hunsdon House	England	*Folk Dances of the British Isles*
Igüiris, Las	Mexico	*Folk Dances of the United States and Mexico*
In the Garden	Russia	*Folk Dances of European Countries*
In the Green Meadow	Czechoslovakia	''
Irish Lilt	Ireland	*Folk Dances of the British Isles*
Irish Long Dance	Ireland	''
Jabado	France	*Folk Dances of European Countries*
Jarabe Tapatío, El	Mexico	*Folk Dances of the United States and Mexico*
Kanafaska	Moravia	*Folk Dances of European Countries*
Kerenski	Finland	*Folk Dances of Scandinavia*
Kolo	Serbia	*Folk Dances of European Countries*
Koróboushka	Russia	''
Kynkkaliepakko	Finland	*Folk Dances of Scandinavia*
Ladies to the Center and Back to the Bar	America	*Folk Dances of the United States and Mexico*
Lady Round the Lady	America	''
Lauterbach	Switzerland	*Folk Dances of European Countries*
Life on the Ocean Wave	America	*Folk Dances of the United States and Mexico*
Little Four Dance	Norway	*Folk Dances of Scandinavia*
Little Man in a Fix	Denmark	''
Matlanchines, Los	Mexico	*Folk Dances of the United States and Mexico*
New Bavarian, The	Germany	*Folk Dances of European Countries*
Norwegian Varsovienne	Norway	*Folk Dances of Scandinavia*
Oxen Dance	Sweden	''
Oxford Minuet	America	*Folk Dances of the United States and Mexico*
Paw Paw Patch	America	''

Dance	Country	Volume
Radiko	Finland	*Folk Dances of Scandinavia*
Reinlendar	Norway	''
Ril	Norway	''
Row Well, Ye Mariners	England	*Folk Dances of the British Isles*
Rufty Tufty	England	''
Rugen	Norway	*Folk Dances of Scandinavia*
Rye Waltz	America	*Folk Dances of the United States and Mexico*
Schuhplattler — A Couple Dance	Germany	*Folk Dances of European Countries*
Schuhplattler — A Dance for Two Men	Germany	''
Seven Steps	Germany	''
Shoo Fly	America	*Folk Dances of the United States and Mexico*
Sleights Sword Dance	England	*Folk Dances of the British Isles*
Straw Cutter, The	Germany	*Folk Dances of European Countries*
Stoupic, Le	France	''
Stupid One Turning Quickly	Germany	''
Swedish Schottische	Sweden	*Folk Dances of Scandinavia*
Swedish Varsovienne	Sweden	''
Swiss Schottische	Switzerland	*Folk Dances of European Countries*
Take a Little Peek	America	*Folk Dances of the United States and Mexico*
Tantoli	Norway	*Folk Dances of Scandinavia*
Viejitos, Los	Mexico	*Folk Dances of the United States and Mexico*
Virgencita, La	Mexico	''
Weggis Dance	Switzerland	*Folk Dances of European Countries*

BIBLIOGRAPHY

Bovard, John F., and Cozens, Frederick W. *Tests and Measurements in Physical Education.* Philadelphia: W. B. Saunders, 1938.

Brand, John. *Observations on Popular Antiquities.* London: Chatto and Windus, Piccadily, 1877.

Briggs, Thomas H. *Secondary Education.* New York: The Macmillan Company, 1933.

Chambers, Robert. *The Book of Days,* 2 vols. Philadelphia: J. P. Lippincott Co., 1864.

Clarke, H. Harrison. *The Application of Measurement to Health and Physical Education.* New York: Prentice-Hall, Inc., 1945.

Encyclopedia Americana. New York: Americana Corporation, 1945 Edition.

Encyclopedia Britannica, 14th ed, Vol. 19. Chicago: Encyclopedia Britannica, 1939.

15 Exitos Rancheros Mexicanos. Mexico, D. F.: Promotora Hispana Americana de Musica, S. A.

Garrett, Henry E. *Statistics in Psychology and Education.* New York: Longmans, Green and Co., 1926.

Geary, Marjorie Crane. *Folk Dances of Czechoslovakia.* New York: A. S. Barnes and Company, 1927.

Glassow, Ruth B., and Broer, Marion R. *Measuring Achievement in Physical Education.* Philadelphia: W. B. Saunders Company, 1938.

Horst, Louis. *Pre-Classic Dance Forms.* New York: The Dance Observer, 1937.

Kinney, Troy, and Kinney, Margaret West. *The Dance; Its Place in Art and Life.* New York: Tudor Publishing Co., 1935.

Kirstein, Lincoln. *The Book of the Dance.* Garden City, New York: Garden City Publishing Co., Inc., 1942.

Kozman, Hilda Chute, Cassidy, Rosalind, and Jackson, Chester O. *Methods in Physical Education.* Philadelphia: W. B. Saunders Company, 1947.

Lincoln, Jeanette. *The Festival Book.* New York: A. S. Barnes and Company, 1929.

McCloy, Charles Harold. *Tests and Measurements in Physical Education.* New York: F. S. Crofts and Company, 1939.

Report of the United States Office of Education Committee on Wartime Physical Fitness for Colleges and Universities. *Physical Fitness for Students in Colleges and Universities.* Washington, D. C.: United States Government Printing Office, 1943.

Sachs, Curt. *World History of the Dance.* New York: W. W. Norton and Company, Inc., 1937.

Scott, M. Gladys, and French, Esther. *Better Teaching Through Testing.* New York: A. S. Barnes and Company, 1945.

Shambaugh, Mary Effie. *Folk Dances for Boys and Girls.* New York: A. S. Barnes and Company, 1929.

————. *Folk Festivals for Schools and Playgrounds.* New York: A. S. Barnes and Company, 1932.

Sharp, Cecil J. *The Country Dance Book,* 5 vols. London: Novello and Company, Ltd., 1909-1918.

Sharp, Cecil J., *et al*. *The Morris Book*, 5 vols. London: Novello and Company, Ltd., 1911-1924.

Strutt, Joseph. *The Sports and Pastimes of the People of England*. London: Thomas Tegg, 73, Cheapside, 1838.

The New International Encyclopedia, Second Edition. New York: Dodd, Mead and Company, 1915.

The World Book Encyclopedia. Chicago: W. F. Quarrie and Company, 1937.

Toor, Frances. *A Treasury of Mexican Folkways*. New York: Crown Publishers, 1947.

Toynbee, Arnold J. *A Study of History*. London: Oxford University Press, 1934.

Urlin, Ethel L. *Dancing Ancient and Modern*. London: Simpkin, Marshall, Hamilton, Kent and Co., Ltd., 1913.

Vuillier, Gaston. *A History of Dancing*. New York: D. Appleton-Century Company, 1897.

Walsh, William S. *Curiosities of Popular Custom*. Philadelphia: J. B. Lippincott Company, 1925.

Williams, Jesse Feiring, Dambach, John I, and Schwendener, Norma. *Methods in Physical Education*. Philadelphia: W. B. Saunders Company, 1937.

DANCE

A Books for Libraries Collection

Ashihara, Eiryo. **The Japanese Dance.** 1964

Bowers, Faubion. **Theatre in the East.** 1956

Brinson, Peter. **Background to European Ballet.** 1966

Causley, Marguerite. **An Introduction to Benesh Movement Notation.** 1967

Devi, Ragini. **Dances of India.** 1962

Duggan, Ann Schley, Jeanette Schlottmann and Abbie Rutledge. **The Teaching of Folk Dance.** Volume 1. 1948

_____. **Folk Dances of Scandinavia.** Volume 2. 1948

_____. **Folk Dances of European Countries.** Volume 3. 1948

_____. **Folk Dances of the British Isles.** Volume 4. 1948

_____. **Folk Dances of the United States and Mexico.** Volume 5. 1948

Duncan, Irma. **Duncan Dancer.** 1966

Dunham, Katherine. **A Touch of Innocence.** 1959

Emery, Lynne Fauley. **Black Dance in the United States from 1619 to 1970.** 1972

Fletcher, Ifan Kyrle, Selma Jeanne Cohen and Roger Lonsdale. **Famed for Dance.** 1960

Gautier, Théophile. **The Romantic Ballet as Seen by Théophile Gautier.** 1932

Genthe, Arnold. **Isadora Duncan.** 1929

Hall, J. Tillman. **Dance! A Complete Guide to Social, Folk, & Square Dancing.** 1963

Jackman, James L., ed. **Fifteenth Century Basse Dances.** 1964

Joukowsky, Anatol M. **The Teaching of Ethnic Dance.** 1965

Kahn, Albert Eugene. **Days with Ulanova.** 1962

Karsavina, Tamara. **Theatre Street.** 1950

Lawson, Joan. **European Folk Dance.** 1953

Martin, John. **The Dance.** 1946

Sheets-Johnstone, Maxine. **The Phenomenology of Dance.** 1966